Praise for

A Feast at the Beach

"With a clever pen and sincere style, Widmaier is brilliant at wiping away all the cliché's you've seen all too often on TV about life in St. Tropez.
In **A Feast at the Beach,** *you'll find yourself immersed in the Provence of the '60s, a universe that evokes both the novels of Marcel Pagnol and the photographs of Robert Doisneau. The author shares with us stories filled with humor and tenderness....*
To read Widmaier's **A Feast At The Beach** *is also a bit like walking into a Provençal kitchen, with its bright colors and smells of lavender, thyme, rosemary and bay."*

Sophie Fung
French Morning magazine

"In every jewel-like chapter William captures the essence of what it was to be a child in a Provence that is passing from memory. My children experienced, summer after summer, the same world that he inhabited, although a decade earlier and deep in the interior. In **A Feast at the Beach** *I find our own summer memories of beach and* **gouter,** *of bouilliabaise and aioli reflected in his evocative writing. A lovely book."*

Georgeanne Brennan
Author of *A Pig in Provence* and
The Food and Flavors of Haute Provence.

2 —

If you were lucky enough

To have grandparents who lived in St. Tropez,

Lessons in La Joie de Vivre were all around

&

Life was a feast at the beach.

Dedicated to my wife Tiaré, who believed in my writing,
sometimes more than I did.

ᵃFeast
at the Beach

William Widmaier

Copyright registered at the Library of Congress, United States of America.
Registration number: TXu 1-628-655

Library of Congress Control Number: 2010931485
ISBN-13: 978-0-615-38414-6

A Feast at the Beach soft-cover first edition 2010

For more information about special discounts for bulk purchases, please contact 3L Publishing at 916.300.8012 or log onto our website at www.3LPublishing.com.

Text set in Palatino
Author's photograph on back cover by Tiaré Ferrari
Printed in the United States of America

TABLE OF CONTENTS

PROLOGUE

the Berries *of* Seduction

THE *CAFÉ CRÈME* WAS HOT AND BITTER AND TASTED DELICIOUS. My brother and I sat in front of the roadside café and sipped our coffees that were more *café* than *crème*, breathed in the berry-scented air, and said nothing. Every once in a while a truck would come roaring through, downshifting as it approached the hamlet, accelerating as soon as it crossed the empty intersection. The hamlet was in the middle of the green, green Normandy countryside, resting midway between Paris and the ocean.

We were both tired from the long flight from San Francisco. This was the first time I had returned to France in a long time, and while tired, I was also exhilarated – such that I could not have slept even if I wanted to. This was my wife's first visit to France and every few moments I would peek at the car, looking for the telltale sign of a confused head rising, indicating she had woken from her nap in the backseat.

My brother had slept on and off since we picked up the car at Charles de Gaulle airport, rousing as we approached the hamlet as if he knew I desired to stop for a coffee. As we rolled into the hamlet, I spotted the café, and I made my intentions known – and he grunted a half-awake agreement.

We drank our cups and savored every bitter drop for these were not ordinary coffees; rather they were long, lost friends welcoming our return; the sugar cubes on the saucers somehow smiling at us. The fact that we had finally managed our return to France had a profound affect on us. We had not grown up in France, but we had visited often enough as children, staying with our grandparents, and going to school for up to three months at a time. These stays formed the most cherished and pleasurable moments of my childhood, and I can only assume it was the same for my brother. Yet, despite all these wonderful memories, I had not returned since our teen years.

The Earth had circled the sun 14 times since I had parted from this country last, when the emptiness began, over the years growing, and sometimes becoming painful. Liberal applications of French wine, food, music and artifacts soothed it temporarily, but within days it would be festering again. Now I was back, and over the next few weeks I would gradually discover that France was like a lover who became bitter if ignored or scorned. She wanted my attention and my presence. She had seduced and lodged herself in my soul during my childhood and had refused to leave.

Thank god.

When our cups were empty, and I was ready to go I looked at my brother.

"Ready?"

"Yep."

I turned to the waitress as we stood to leave.

"*Merci.*"

She nodded but with great reservation. *She was France*, and *She* was not quite sure whether to accept us back yet.

We continued toward the coast, toward Mont St. Michel as if it were a magical destination, which in fact it was. I had been there before, when I was 14, and it had loomed like an ancient enchanted kingdom out of the fog and salt-grass marshes. It had beguiled me then, and no matter how many pictures of it I had seen since, I was always struck by its mystery and beauty.

My wife woke up with a smile as I drove down the road through the green fields and hills with small ancient castles.

"William, I absolutely love the way the air smells here. It's been full of berries since we arrived."

Magic was in the air.

Another seduction was beginning.

CHAPTER I

the Red Scarf

I REMEMBER THE FIRST TIME I WENT TO FRANCE. We arrived at my grandparent's house late in the evening, and I could barely keep my eyes open. The only thing that kept me awake was that I knew Christmas presents awaited, and as every four-year-old knows: Christmas presents from your Grandparents are always extraordinary. I had visions of big, magical gifts; something vaguely to do with trains or cars, and it would have tracks or rails and engines; and it would make noise and move under its own steam.

We were ushered into what should have been a strange house, as it did not resemble anything I had previously experienced in the States. Instead, the house was warm and friendly and smelled somehow comforting, putting me right at ease. We gathered in the living room, crowded with a grand, old antique cabinet filled with family heirlooms, some chairs, a Christmas tree, and my grandmother's sewing machine in the corner. The introductions went by in a blur, as it was not the focus of my attention. My older brother Stephan and I pressed, as children do, toward receiving our presents, and eventually the time came. There was only one package for me, and it was suspiciously small. I eagerly opened my gift – it was a red scarf. I'm sure I did not keep the disappointment off my face, but when you are four-years-old maybe you have that right. I thought it was the only Christmas gift I was to receive from my grandparents.

That night my mother put my brother and me to bed, side by side, in my uncle's room. She opened a nearby window to "let the air in" and left a night-light on for us. The next morning, I awoke with at least 25 to 50 mosquito bites that covered my head, neck and arms. My brother was similarly attacked, but with about half the damage. The adults had a fit, fearing for my life, but somehow I survived. My life-long battle with mosquitoes had begun.

My grandparents lived in a house dating from the 17th century. It shared the north wall with the back of a small church, *La Chapelle St. Joseph*. You can see it in Henri Matisse's 1904 painting of the same name. The house had been built in stages, the lowest part consisting of one room for the priest of the church to live in, then 200 years ago, several other rooms were added as well as a stable, and then 100 years or so later the upper bedrooms. The house dripped with history and secret lore – and I loved it for this. It was not a fancy house as it was really just a caretaker's home for the small church. Next to it was the grand *Maison de Maître*, the always-empty property owner's mansion that dominated the estate. Behind the house was a large backyard and, beyond that, vineyards. The front of the house looked over vineyards, the town of St. Tropez, and the gulf beyond.

The smells of my grandparent's house were a combination of kitchen aromas heavy in fresh herbs, especially basil, parsley and the scent of tomato leaves when bent or broken. And Ricard, and wine, the special wine of St. Tropez my grandfather would purchase by bringing down to the co-op his large five-gallon glass jugs wrapped in woven straw. There were the smells of the wax-rubbed wood furniture, the *Savon de Marseille* used in the kitchen and bathrooms, the mustiness, especially in the secret passageway and the wine cave, the starched sun-dried sheets, lavender sachets, and the vineyards that surrounded the house whose aroma became ever more pungent as we neared the harvest season. It was the smell of the spiral punks we burned at night to keep the mosquitoes away, and the wild flowers and herbs drifting down from the forest on the hills a kilometer away. It was the salty breeze from the Mediterranean coming in through the windows, and the hint of machine oil from my grandfather's garage. Add to all this, another essence I can best categorize as history. It took many years for me to isolate one of the key aromas that made up this fragrance. It's frankincense. The furniture and walls in my grandparent's house was imbued with the smell of frankincense, though I never saw it being burned. Rather it's the product of hundreds of years of accumulation from previous tenants, beginning with the priests in the 17th century.

One night, my grandmother awakened us at around 2:00 a.m. We put on our Christmas scarves over our pajamas and were rushed downstairs and outside. It was snowing – a very rare event in St. Tropez. We marveled as the snow fell down, and then returned sleepily to our beds and pleasant dreams.

Not once did I ever have a nightmare while sleeping in my grandparent's house.

In the morning, the snow was gone, melting at first light.

When we returned to the States after that first trip, I took my red scarf with me. I cherished it for all it meant, keeping it through my teen years, past my parents' divorce, and even when I moved out on my own, though by then it had shrunk from too many washes and was too ratty to wear.

I kept it in my underwear drawer.

It was comforting just to have it.

Mémé's Sleeping Potion

This worked for me as a child, and it still works for me today.

> 1 1/2 cups of milk, preferably organic or raw whole milk
> 1 drop of vanilla extract
> 1 teaspoon of chestnut honey or lavender honey

Warm milk slowly, until it is too hot to touch. Do not let it boil. Remove any skin that may have formed and pour hot milk into a classic French coffee bowl. Add vanilla and stir in honey until dissolved. Sip slowly while thinking pleasant thoughts.

Note: When you know you will need something extra strong you can add 1 oz of Marc, Armagnac or Cognac, stirring it in with the honey.

CHAPTER II

the War Hero

MY GRANDFATHER, LOUIS, OR PÉPÉ AS WE CALLED HIM, CAME FROM PEASANT STOCK. He stole my grandmother's heart and married outside his class; my grandmother being blueblood French descended from the Dauphins of Auvergne. The marriage caused quite a stir, and so to get away from it all they moved from St. Etienne in central France to St. Tropez on the coast of the Mediterranean.

Pépé was not a tall man, maybe 5'7", always fit, bald on top as many Frenchmen are, and moved briskly, like a man with purpose who knew exactly what he was doing. He was a career Navy man, though not an officer. He was an engineer working his whole life in the French naval torpedo research facility near St. Tropez the locals called simply *l'Usine*. He did not wear a naval uniform, but he wore a uniform of sorts, the bleu de travail, the traditional French workman's uniform of blue pants and shirt or blue jumpsuit, with blue canvas shoes.

Wherever we went together throughout Provence

people would recognize him.

"Hey Louis, how are you? Where's the bicycle?"

My grandfather was a war hero, but not the kind they give medals to. During World War II, the wives and children of the engineers and officers who worked at *l'Usine* moved up together into central France.

The men felt that their families would be safer away from the coast – and in an area with more agriculture and fewer Germans. The Germans had a strong interest in the work being done there and insisted the officers and engineers stay at the facility, steep on cots, and the Germans would push hard for torpedo design and development to continue. Much to the frustration of the Germans, the men stalled and much of their work just went in circles.

My grandfather and the other men were happy their families were far away so the Germans could not easily use them for extra pressure.

Every couple of months, my grandfather would collect all the men's salaries and get on his bicycle, a bulging envelope tucked into his shirt, and ride into central France. Sometimes he would be riding while the resistance fighters and the Germans were taking potshots at each other, or while the front lines were moving up and down the South of France. Dressed in his *bleu de travail* and cycling cap, carrying a significant amount of money, he rode past checkpoints, and on occasion he kept his head down and pedaled at a steady pace while he heard the bullets whiz and felt grenades explode near him. He approached it all with the idea that it was normal to see a man riding a bicycle in France, and so if he just ignored the troops and resistance fighters they would ignore him.

He did this ride because he was the best cyclist in St. Tropez. He did this ride so that the dozen families of his co-workers and officers, including his own wife and first child, would have enough money to buy food and bare necessities to survive. He did this ride a dozen times, each ride being approximately 1,000 kilometers, round trip.

After the war, my grandfather continued to ride, taking weekend trips throughout the South of France, stopping in small villages for lunch or a drink and conversation, resulting in an immense circle of casual friends.

Once France was liberated, there were still severe food shortages, so my grandfather learned the arcane art of gathering mushrooms to supplement the family's meager food supply. Years later, when we stayed with my grandparents, Pépé would take us mushroom hunting. This consisted of waiting ideally about three days after a rain, and then going for a walk in the woods. Sometimes when the weekend was four or five days after the rain, we would still try. We would only go to select forests my grandfather knew would produce results. We would stroll through the forests with Pépé dispatching us to look under particular trees. If we found anything, we called out but never touched the mushrooms until he arrived, as there were a variety of mushrooms, some of which are extremely poisonous. When he arrived, he would examine them and pass judgment. Often we would find Cèpes, and on good outings would fill our straw baskets full. I remember a particular outing where we found some Cèpes about 12-inches wide and an inch-and-a-quarter thick. We brought them home and my grandmother sautéed them in butter and garlic as if they were steaks, filling the kitchen with a phenomenal nutty essence that was two parts earth, one part spice. With this dinner we drank our usual watered cup of wine, about five parts water to one part wine, that my grandfather insisted was our right as young Frenchman.

Pépé would often take us on drives, showing us old Roman ruins and numerous natural wonders, stopping at bars where he invariably knew the owner, and buying us Oranginas or having my brother and I split a beer in glasses first filled with a quarter inch of grenadine, creating a wonderful slightly sweet rose-colored drink. The fact that it was a real beer and sanctioned by an adult, and we were drinking it at a bar, added to the thrill.

One weekend when I was 11, Pépé took us mountain climbing. We climbed up a small rocky limestone mountain covered in *Garrigue* – the *Provençal* scrub made up of scraggly oaks, thyme, sage, rosemary, miscellaneous other brush, and in the spring fields of red poppies. We climbed and took occasional stops to sip water laced with a few drops of wine out of our leather wine sacks, and to chew on raw salt pork or suck on a sugar cube for energy.

After several hours, still several hundred feet from the top, we stopped at a hermit's cave. This was the most advanced cave I'd ever seen, with a door in the front and running water from a catch above the cave. We had to politely wait a dozen paces away from the hermit's cave door while my grandfather inquired if the hermit was talking today. He was – and we were invited in. To my surprise, even the hermit knew my grandfather. Somehow, a hermit who had an on again off again vow of silence, living in a cave near the top of a mountain knew my grandfather. I could never get from my grandfather how it was that they knew each other. We stayed 10 minutes and then continued our climb.

Once we reached the top, Pépé gave us an instant lesson in rappelling and launched us down the steep back-side of the mountain. We made it down and to the car in less than half the time, and headed home exhausted yet triumphant. We were now mountain climbers.

Pépé saw his job as to not just raise us, his *petit-fils*, into men, but into Frenchmen, and that included learning how to sail.

Pépé, being a naval engineer, built his own sailboat. It was a small, white, wooden catamaran built not for speed but for strength and stability. The boat's name was *Mouette*. On summer weekends, we would get up in the morning and look out our bedroom window at the bay. If there was only blue and no white showing, we knew there was not enough wind for sailing. If the whitecaps were more than 50 percent of blue then Pépé considered it too windy to go out. Anywhere in-between, and we had a good chance of convincing him to take us out. We would go down to the moored boat, load up a lunch, and sail out onto the bay. Sometimes we would beach her at *La Plage de Bouillabaisse*, one of St. Tropez's less-famous beaches, where the rest of the family would be, and we would join them for lunch before we took her back out again. I used to collect Matchbox cars, and my grandfather would have me take one along and put the car in the center of the boat where it would sit without moving, and he would call out, "See! See how stable she is!"

One hot summer day my mother, brother, both grandparents and I headed to the beach. We were going to a special beach, different than our usual. We parked the car, and each person loaded up for the walk among the rocks to the hidden beach. My grandfather gave me the honor of carrying the bottle of wine. The wine had been chilled and the bottle was sweating. It was an unmarked, clear, thick glass bottle, which is the type that sits on the table and is reused over and over. I was proud to be the wine carrier. As we crossed the gravel parking area, I could smell the salt of the ocean and the sharp smell of the beach canes that grow in the south; I could hear the loud singing of the Mediterranean cicadas, the French call them *cigales*. The bottle began to slip in my hands. Though I tried to hold the bottle tighter it just continued to slide through my now wet little hands. As it slipped out I reached down to catch it only to have it slide out again. The bottle hit the ground and shattered in that familiar sound that we all know and cringe upon hearing. The smell of wine immediately filled the air. I knelt down as if gathering the pieces of glass could somehow save some of the wine.

Pépé turned and looked at what I had done.

"Ah no! No! No! No! It's not possible!"

My thoughts exactly. I had been given the place of honor and had failed miserably.

"I can't believe you dropped the bottle."

Abject anguish.

"You're going back and getting another one."

I began calculating the distance it would be to walk back to the house to get another bottle. It was a long way, and I wasn't exactly sure of the route. I was scared, very scared, but willing.

My grandmother, we called her Mémé, intervened like an angel from heaven.

"Louis, can't you see it was an accident? You're

making the child miserable. You can manage the afternoon without your wine."

And she took him by the hand and led him off. She had an absolutely amazing power over the man.

He loved her deeply.

Pépé was French to the core. He was a man of the people and disdained aristocratic airs. He loved his wine and believed a glass with your meal was every Frenchman's right. I never saw him drunk. He ate his meal using his Opinel pocketknife while we all used the standard silverware. When he liked something, he would give you a thumbs up and say, *"Chapeau!"* He could swear a blue streak, which usually resulted in my brother and me bursting out laughing, trying to remember and recreate the memorable turn of phrases he used. He was a magician in his youth doing shows for fun in the town square with my young mother as an assistant. He retired from the Navy with honors at a formal ceremony that made the newspapers. A torpedo he helped design and build still sits in the museum in the *Citadelle de St. Tropez*. He refused to fly, stating he did not trust airplanes. He continued riding his bicycle, against doctor's orders, into his late seventies.

He did not tell me the story of his World War II rides until the last time I saw him.

Mémé buried him in his cycling outfit.

A Few Provençal Libations

These drinks are all warm weather fare,
best served while out on the terrace,
basking in the Mediterranean sun,
or while at a Café off the town square when
you are taking a break from some intense
mid-afternoon games of Pétanque.

Monaco

Refreshing, slightly sweet, pink in hue,
especially the foamy head. It takes the sharp
edge off any beer.

> 1 bottle of a good pale beer, such as
> Kronenbourg 1664 or Stella Artois
> 2 tablespoons grenadine syrup

Pour grenadine into a tall, chilled glass. Add
beer, tilting glass and letting it slide down
the side to minimize what will be a big pink
head of foam. Add more beer after you've
sipped and made room.

The first sip is the sweetest.

Panaché

This is a very crisp, clean drink with a relatively low alcohol level. Good for when you need to keep your head clear, but still want something refreshing from the bar.

Warning, it goes down very easily.

> 1/2 bottle of a good pale beer, such as Kronenbourg 1664 or Stella Artois
> 1/2 bottle of French-style sparkling lemonade, or lemon soda.

 Mix evenly cold beer with sparkling lemonade in a tall, chilled glass.

Mauresque

Most people are familiar with the classic Ricard – the anis-flavored liquor served with ice and a large jug of cold water that is de rigueur on hot days anywhere in the South of France. As a child, it was all around me, but not something ever served to children. It is strong in both flavor and alcoholic strength. When I returned to France as a young man, I became fond of the occasional Ricard. Then, one day while sitting on the terrace at the Carlton, while working at the Cannes Film Festival, my good friend Stephen Salinger suggested he order us drinks, and I tasted my first *Mauresque*. I was an instant convert. Very seldom seen in the States, this one is perfect for sipping while people watching on a hot *Provençal* afternoon.

> 1 large chilled glass
> 1 jug of chilled water
> Plenty of ice
> 1 oz Ricard (or your favorite pastis)
> 1 oz orgeat syrup (a sweet syrup
> made from almonds)

Pour Ricard and orgeat into glass. Fill with large ice cubes. Add water. Stir gently. Sip slowly, feigning great languor, smiling as if you own the world, and sporting a fine pair of sunglasses.

CHAPTER III

*the*Dimwitted Little American

MY FIRST WEEK AT SCHOOL IN ST. TROPEZ WAS A MISERY. On my second trip to France, when I was about six years old, the fact that I would be going to school there hit me the day we arrived as my parents immediately took Stephan and me to the school and enrolled us.

The fact that I had never written a word of French did not concern my parents.

"What better way to learn?" my father explained.

The fact that I did not know a single other child at the school didn't concern them either.

These were important facts as far as I was concerned, yet my father assured me that I would manage. Now I love my father, but when I was a child sometimes his lack of empathy seemed somehow callous. That he was always right just made things worse.

For me things went from bad to worse. My brother's class, three grades ahead of me despite our two years of difference – just because he started school a year early, like me, but then had the audacity to skip up a grade – was, of all things, going on a ski trip for a week and leaving the following day. In the excitement, all attention shifted to my ecstatic brother. He would need a bonnet, heavy jacket, mittens and thick socks – ski goggles too. He already had his scarf.

For me, a *cahier*, the traditional French notebook with black-and-white-patterned hardcover and strangely blue-lined paper inside. With this, my first fountain pen, a pencil, eraser and a little plastic zip bag to hold them in.

The next morning we brought my brother to the town square, loaded him up in the bus with dozens of other kids, and waved him off.

I was now alone.

My parents and grandmother took me to school and dropped me off a few minutes before class was to start. I found my way to the classroom and introduced myself to the teacher, and let her know my concerns on my ability to write in French. She sniffed and told me that since I could speak and write English – and could obviously speak French – then there was no reason I could not learn to also write in French as well. The room quickly filled up – and I discovered that our class, in fact our whole school, was segregated. We only had boys in our school, the girls went to a school next door.

Class started promptly at 8:15 a.m. I was introduced to the other students as *notre petit étudiant Américain*, our little American student, and everyone, please, was to help me learn and get up to speed. The way she described me, you would think I was slightly retarded simply by the fact that I was American. Her pointing out my small size didn't help. I was small for my age and continued this way until my late teens where I grew suddenly with such speed that I had stretch marks on the side of my torso. To my increasing dismay the teacher's introduction and excuses for my assumed dimness brought me a bunch of dark looks from the other boys.

The first recess was at 10:0 a.m., and we were required to go outside. We had a small yard shared by our class, the grade above, and the grade below. This playground was separated from a second yard reserved for the now-absent upper classes by a low, simple fence. In no time, the bullies from my class gathered with the bullies from the class just above and began pointing my way. I did my best to be invisible. Fortunately, recess was only 15 minutes, and we were back in class before trouble could start. At noon we were let out, my parents picked me up, and we drove up the hill to my grandparent's house. I did my best to make my misery clear to them, but I was instead reminded that my parents were leaving that afternoon for Belgium, and after that they would return back to the States and, by the way, my grandfather would pick me up after school.

Lunch was two hours long and then back to class until 5:00 p.m. That night, I cried my misery onto my grandmother's shoulder. My older brother Stephan, who did not come close to suffering my size issues, was in the Alps skiing; my parents were gone; and I was being locked-up with a bunch of bigger boys who all hated me. My grandmother explained to me that it wasn't that they hated me, it was just that an American was somewhat mythic to them. They had probably never met one, and they just didn't know what to make of me. Well, I knew hostility when I saw it, nothing mysterious or mythic about it, no sir.

The next day the class smart aleck went too far with some remark during a lesson, and the teacher walked over to his desk, grabbed him by the ear, and dragged him to the front of the class. She pulled his pants down in front of the class, bent him over her desk, and started spanking him. My mouth hung open in shock, and a scream of terror was barely held in check. This was school discipline? No. This was insane! I could never survive such an event if it were to happen to me. I would die of embarrassment and shame. Not only that, this kid had red Speedo-style underwear, what would they make of my classic white Fruit-of-the-Looms?

At recess that day a bright, red-haired, freckle-faced kid named Pierre shyly came over to talk to me. He said he had told his mother about me, and that she had suggested he talk to me, and so, he had some questions. This was followed that day and for the next several days, with a barrage of questions about America. Some sensible, some outlandish, including, "I thought all American's were big?" and, "Does everybody wear pistols?" to the inevitable, upon hearing I lived in Los Angeles next to Hollywood, "Do you know any stars?" Other kids came with their questions too, and Pierre controlled these recess events as if he were my agent. If anything this attention from some of the smarter, geekier segment of the class bothered the bullies even more. Trouble was brewing, I could see it and feel it, yet somehow I managed to live through that first week.

Our school schedule was affected by the market day schedule of St. Tropez. I discovered this was common in all small towns in France, designed so the kids could help their parents either man a stand and sell at market or help shop for the week's groceries. In St. Tropez back then, market day was on Tuesdays, with the market taking place on half of the Place des Lices and going from about 8:00 a.m. to noon. Thus, we had no school Tuesdays until 2:00 p.m. We made up this time by having to go to school on Saturday from 8:15 a.m. till noon. Now on Saturday, St. Tropez had its *foire*, which, like the market day, had most of the same food vendors, but was also made up of outside vendors coming to town to sell their wares, taking up both sides of the Place de Lices and going till around 1:00 p.m. The fact that the same town vendors went on Tuesday and Saturdays – but we had to go to school on one day and not the other never made much sense to me but heck, I was the dimwitted *petit Americain* so what did I know?

My brother, thankfully, returned that Sunday with tales of adventure and fun. Apparently his class had embraced him as some great American John Wayne cool guy. This positioning was greatly enhanced by a late night adventure he had. One of the kids, the smart aleck of his grade, had a habit of bursting into the dormitory he shared with half a dozen other boys and jumping from bed to bed while screaming. He would do this in the middle of the night after lights out while everybody was sleeping. Obviously, all the kids in my brother's dormitory were unhappy about this foolishness and threats were issued; but, like all smart alecks, a threat is no better than a dare. A half-hour later, once everybody had gone to sleep, he would come through again. My brother, who has never been in a fight in his life, other than to beat up yours truly, found this behavior unacceptable. On the third night of this late-night annoyance, my brother got up, intercepted the kid in the hall just outside his dormitory room, grabbed him by the front of his PJs and slammed him against the wall, literally picking him up off the ground. He told him the next time he came into the room and disturbed their sleep he would be thrown out the window. By now all the kids were in the hall to witness. The American had spoken and with force. The kids from my brother's dorm room cheered as the smart aleck ran to his room in terror. My brother's reputation was made.

This was all fine and well, and I was happy for him, but unlike him, I was just a small kid, "Shrimp," as he would call me repeatedly over my objections, and my doom was coming at school in the next day or so. I told my brother of my impending fist-induced tenderizing – and he shrugged it off, saying I was exaggerating and these French kids were really nice, didn't I think so? Great, wasn't this what older brothers were for, defending their little brothers?

The next morning at recess, the bullies gathered round me. My new friend Pierre, to his credit, stayed at my side and told them where to go. No help. Pierre was the same size as I was, and the bigger bullies weren't impressed. A crowd started gathering, they could smell a fight, or more like it, a one-sided pounding. Seconds before the first punch was thrown, one of the older kids on the other side of the fence called out to the bullies.

"Are you guys crazy?"

"What?"

"Don't mess with him!"

"What, the little dimwit? Why not?"

"He's the American's little brother!"

"So?

"Are you nuts? He's like John Wayne, man. He's

super strong and tough. He almost threw Philippe out the second-story window just because Philippe pissed him off. You mess with his little brother and who knows what he'll do to you."

"Oh."

"I'm serious, don't mess with the little brother. You'll regret it."

By now a crowd of the older kids were at the fence all nodding in agreement. The bullies had all gone white. They knew Philippe, and he was much bigger than they were, and he had a reputation too. If this John Wayne kid had almost thrown him out a window, what would he do to them? The lead bully turned from the fence and patted me on the shoulder.

"It's alright, we were just joking. Right? Everything's OK? No harm done, right?"

I nodded yes, and they moved away in obvious relief. The older boys across the fence looked at me and grinned, giving me the thumbs up. Disaster had been averted; I had a new lease on life.

I was never bothered again by any of the kids in the school.

At lunch, when I told my brother about my being saved by John Wayne, he thought it was hilarious, having no idea what had happened, despite being in the older kids yard at the time.

When he stopped laughing, my eight-year-old big brother, who had never been in a fight and has never been in a fight to this day, paused for a bit and told me seriously, rest assured, if the bullies had actually started beating me up he would have jumped the fence immediately and taught them a lesson.

For all my misery and misadventures, I did gain something of incalculable value at that school: Pierre, my five-and-a-half-year-old, freckle-faced, red-headed agent, became my best friend. We hung out together every time I came to France, or at least until I was eleven years old.

La Salade Campagnarde Provençale

Simple and delicious, this basic rustic salad recipe is almost exactly how my grandmother made it.

La Vinaigrette
1/2 teaspoon *Herbes de Provence*
1/2 teaspoon Dijon mustard
1 teaspoon lemon juice (preferably fresh squeezed)
1 tablespoon red-wine vinegar
1/2 cup good-quality, extra-virgin olive oil

La Salade
1 shallot
2 cloves garlic
1.5 oz of salt pork or thick-cut pancetta
1 large butter lettuce
Mediterranean sea salt to taste

First make the vinaigrette:
Take *Herbes de Provence* (if the mix does not include Lavender flowers, it is not a true *Herbes de Provence* in my opinion) and put them in a mortar and pestle and crush slightly to bring the aromas out before placing them in a small mixing bowl. Add mustard, lemon juice and vinegar and mix

together thoroughly. Add olive oil at a slow dribble while whisking constantly. The oil and vinegar will blend and then fall apart, this is expected, do not worry. The whisking imbues the oil with the other flavors. Salt to taste – recommend no more than a couple pinches. Set aside the vinaigrette.

The Salad:
Slice salt pork into small pieces about 1/4 inch by 1/2 inch, no bigger. Slice the garlic and shallots into thin slices, and then cross chop them once or twice.

Throw salt pork into a small skillet along with a tablespoon of olive oil. Set to medium heat. Stir frequently. As soon as salt pork even hints at browning, add garlic and shallots, and continue to cook, and stir frequently. When salt pork begins to truly take on color (do not over cook), turn off but leave in skillet to keep warm.

Rinse the butter lettuce, break off leaves, and spin them dry in a salad spinner or twirling wire basket. Rip butter leaves into large bite-size pieces and put them all in a large salad bowl. Take still-warm skillet and scrape onto salad, salt pork, shallots and garlic. Let warm oils drip onto the lettuce as well. Strir up the vinaigrette and add just enough to lightly coat the lettuce leaves when tossed, somewhere between

2-4 tablespoons, depending on the amount of lettuce. Toss and serve.

Note: There are as many variations to this salad as there are grandmothers' kitchens. Some add warmed goat cheese, and/or croutons, tomatoes, dried black olives, cucumbers, chunks of tuna, etc. The recipe above is basic and delicious. Start with that and explore as you wish.

CHAPTER IV

the Deepest Well

WHY IS IT, WITH SOME PEOPLE, YOU CAN ONLY REMEMBER THE GOOD THINGS? When we wrote letters she was *Grand Maman Lette*, but in person we just called her Mémé, and I can only remember good things about her.

She was always short, growing shorter as she grew older. Salt-and-pepper hair that eventually became a crown of luxurious white snow; ice-blue eyes that twinkled and smiled most of the time; and a little heavy around the middle, as almost seemed the fashion in earlier generations.

Mémé was often occupied with the various chores related to the preparation of meals, but always with her own unique twist, making a game or adventure of it when she could.

When the grapes in the vineyards out front were ripening, Mémé would send me out with a basket and a mission. I'd fill the basket with the largest, plumpest grape bunches I could find and bring it back to the house, where we would put them in the sink under the cold water to rinse and cool down. Mémé would then take out a hand-powered rotary press she usually used for pureed vegetable soups; but in this case, I would load it with the grapes and start turning. The result was an incredibly heady, fresh-pressed grape juice that often had a small amount of alcohol from the ripening grapes to push you over the edge in case the smell wasn't enough.

Mémé did not cook complicated or fancy French meals as a general rule. What she did make could be considered solid country French. Lentil soup made from scratch, simmered on the stove for what seemed like hours, with little bits of pork fat mixed in, which were melt-in-your-mouth treasures when you found them in your bowl. Puréed vegetable soup made from pressure-steamed fresh vegetables run through the hand mill and seasoned with roast garlic, Mediterranean herbs, fresh-ground black pepper, pinches of sea salt out of the olive-wood box by the stove, and served with a thick slice of butter dropped in the center of your bowl. Sautéed green beans we would snap and soak in the afternoon; traditional ratatouille, homemade mashed potatoes, roasted herb chicken, and the almost nightly *salade campagnarde* tossed with a homemade Dijon vinaigrette. Whatever she did cook always had a sense of freshness and goodness that was uncommon in the States. She never used anything out of a can. She only had a small refrigerator and no freezer. All fruits, vegetables, meats and breads were always fresh, and often a result of going to the market twice a week and the bakery almost every day. The exception was milk. We seemed to have only two choices for milk: fresh and hot out of a friend's cow or ultra pasteurized beyond all reason, where un-refrigerated cartons could spend months on the shelf. The ultra-pasteurizing is a French habit – apparently leftover from hard times during and immediately after the war.

Whenever we had salad, Mémé would make a small pile of the leftover lettuce cores and any fresh vegetable leftovers and send me out to feed the turtles that lived in the old horse stalls around the back of the house, against the chapel.

The stalls had not had horses in them since before my grandparents had moved in, but this didn't prevent them from still smelling like a stable. That smell of several hundred years of stabling horses apparently doesn't go away in just 30 or 40 years. The only thing living in the stalls now were the turtles. The turtles had been living there since my mother was a child, if not longer. These were fairly large turtles, weighing up to several pounds. Sometimes when I brought the lettuce and vegetable leftovers out to them they were nowhere in sight, but seldom did the lettuce not vanish within the next 24 hours. These turtles had no names and were not considered pets, but rather entities that shared our house and, on occasion, our vegetable bounty. Sometimes there were one or two, sometimes three or four. They came and went as they pleased.

After dinner Pépé would go off to read his paper or watch the news, and we would drag a couple of chairs outside the kitchen door and sit with Mémé, look out over the darkening bay, watch the stars come out, feel the evening breeze, and listen to stories she would tell us about the mysteries of the world. Stories from books she'd read by Edgar Casey, Erik Von Daniken and the like. Mémé was very intelligent and widely read. She would pose questions about the mysteries of the world and would patiently listen to our speculations about everything from the building of the pyramids to the ancient Aztecs. She told us old French fables, of werewolves and *La bête du Gévaudan*, of the Knights Templars, and the ancient Phoenicians who plied the southern French coast. She exercised our imaginations and subtly fanned the flames of our curiosity. Sitting outside at night, we would sometimes play 20 questions, traveling in our minds to remote locations envisioning items, artifacts or monuments we all knew and were thus fair game to choose as the object of mystery. It was a game she invariably won. We would play till 9:00 p.m., our bedtime, at which point we would go upstairs, take our bath, close the shutters for the night, climb into our tall, big bed and dream.

If it started to rain, Mémé would have us sing a few rounds of "*Il pleut, il pleut, bergère*" – the sheepherder's song, after which we would listen to the wondrous sounds of the water drops striking the ground, trees, vineyards and grasses. As soon as it was over, we would go out into the fields and take deep breathes of that indescribable "just-after-rain" smell that nature shares with us.

Mémé didn't just prepare us for the future by enlightening us with pieces of world history, she was also the family historian, occasionally traveling but always researching, tracing back our family's line to the Dauphins of Auvergne and their downfall at the hands of Richelieu, and the generations before that, leading ultimately to the long lost civilization of the Celts and Druids.

For all her knowledge of history and the world, or maybe because of it, she'd worry in a fashion that was somehow classic and endearing. When we traveled alone to France, Pépé would pick us up at the Nice airport and drive us to the house, where invariably Mémé would be waiting just outside the kitchen door, wringing her hands in worried anticipation. When we left the scene would often be the same – hands wringing between goodbye waves.

Mémé preferred the kitchen door to the formal entry at the back of the house. She spent the bulk of her time in the kitchen or in the chair she had just outside the kitchen door where she could look out over the vineyards, down into St. Tropez, and beyond to the azure blue gulf. The exception was when she was at her sewing machine, making designer shirts for the fancy men's shop in town.

While Pépé was, beyond a doubt, the man of the house, it was clearly Mémé who actually, quietly and subtly ran the show. She ruled the house with love, compassion, a heartwarming smile, a bit of whining to make you feel guilty when necessary, and, for us, the occasional dragging around by the ear.

While in France Mémé was the rock we orbited around, our fountain of wisdom, our caretaker, our teacher, and the deepest well of love on Earth a child could have.

La magie des oeufs et de l'huile d'olive
(The magic of eggs and olive oil)

Nothing brings to mind the fundamental
pleasures of the *Provençal* kitchen
like those simple magical spreads and
condiments that have at their heart
fresh eggs and olive oil …

La Mayonnaise de Mémé

Mémé would make mayonnaise, as would
on occasion my mother, but never as often
as I would like. Store-bought white mayonnaise just does not compare to homemade.
Not even close. Homemade has a light olive
scent, a golden color, and a smoothness that
is sublime. It is easy to make and stores well
in the refrigerator, if you can keep it from
being consumed! Possibly one of the greatest of simple *Provençal* pleasures are fresh,
deep, red-ripe tomatoes from the garden,
sliced and served with a dollop of homemade mayonnaise.

> 4 egg yolks from fresh high-quality
> eggs
> 4 tablespoons fresh-squeezed lemon
> juice
> 1/2 teaspoon white pepper
> 1/4 teaspoon paprika

1/4 teaspoon Mediterranean sea salt
2 cups extra virgin olive oil
1 tablespoon warm water

In a large bowl, whip egg yolks, lemon juice, white pepper, paprika, and salt until well blended.

While constantly whipping dribble in olive oil and starting with a very slow dribble. When about half olive oil has been used, add the tablespoon of warm water. Continue whipping and dribbling in the olive oil until all the olive oil is used up.

Store in refrigerator in a glass container that seals well.

Note: If you want a lighter mayonnaise, use half olive oil and half grape-seed oil. Pre-mix the oils first.

L'Aioli de Provence

I never like the aioli I get in the States because it frankly just isn't garlicky enough, not to mention the strange things I've seen put in it there, like sugar and relish? I once entered into a futile argument with a waitress when I tried to explain to her that aioli had garlic in it (she said it didn't), and in fact, the word is derived from the old terms for garlic and oil.

Aioli in Provence has a kick. A swift, wide and powerful one. It isn't shy – that's how I make my aioli. The truly old-fashion approach is to use a mortar and pestle to crush the garlic, and while that is the most traditional, I do use the minor short cuts of a garlic press or food processor and a hand-held wire whisk (or mixer when working in volumes), but I shortcut only in my tools, not my ingredients.

2 egg yolks from fresh high-quality eggs
8 garlic cloves (a few more if you wish, but no less!)
1 tablespoon fresh-squeezed lemon juice
1/4 teaspoon Mediterranean sea salt
1 large pinch of saffron threads
1 cup extra virgin olive oil
1 tablespoon warm water

Crush garlic well, the closer to a paste the better, and place in a large bowl. Add egg yolks, lemon juice, salt and crushed, dried saffron threads. Whisk these together until well blended. While constantly whipping, dribble in olive oil and start with a very slow dribble. When half the olive oil has been used, add a tablespoon of warm water. Continue whipping and dribbling in olive oil until all the olive oil is used up. Store in the refrigerator in a glass container that seals well.

While it is also traditional to serve aioli with fish or steamed vegetables, I often use aioli in place of mayonnaise, for example, in sandwiches. It is also delicious as a dip when making steamed artichokes or for dipping French fries.

One of life's simple pleasures is to gather a few friends and just tear pieces off a warm baguette and dip it in a big bowl of aioli set in the middle of the table and enjoy, while sipping a Côtes du Rhône Village, Baux-de-Provence, Côtes de Provence or other local wine.

Note: The aioli is sharpest right after making and mellows over time. I suggest you make it at least two hours before you plan on using it. You will also notice these strange dark spots with an orange halo that starts to show up. These are the tiny bits of saffron threads releasing their wonderful essence into the aioli, and a good sign.

La Rouille

This is a very potent condiment most commonly served with *Provençal* fish soup. It is also quite delicious when used sparingly in a sandwich; it also tastes excellent as a component in a dip, served with a grilled steak or brushed on sardines before grilling.

I've seen various recipes; some featuring soaked bread to thicken it, others using fish broth in the mix. Mine is the classic version, the way I've had it most often in Provence; and fundamentally it becomes a strong aioli with red peppers added. It's very good. As strong as it is, it never lasts more than a couple days in our household, disappearing as if by magic.

1 egg yolk from fresh high-quality eggs
5 garlic cloves
1 tablespoon fresh-squeezed lemon juice
1/8 teaspoon Mediterranean sea salt
1 large pinch of saffron threads
1/2 cup extra virgin olive oil
1 fresh small, sweet red pepper
1 large dried hot red pepper, or 2 smaller dried hot red peppers, or 1 heaping teaspoon of a hot harrisa, such as "Le Phare du Cap" brand.

Crush garlic well and place in a large bowl. Add egg yolk, lemon juice, salt and crushed saffron threads. Use a whisk to whip these together until well blended.

Slice the fresh pepper in half and remove the seeds. Coat the pepper in olive oil then place in a toaster oven or over an open fire and cook until lightly blacken on both sides. Crush to a paste in a mortar and pestle or food processor and add to egg mixture.

Crush dried peppers well in a mortar and pestle or food processor. It should be crushed to a powder. Remove the seeds as best you can by removing cap and pouring them out before crushing. Add crushed peppers (or harrisa if using instead) and whip some more until well blended.

While constantly whipping dribble in olive oil, starting with a very slow dribble. Continue whipping and dribbling in olive oil until all olive oil is used up.

Store in the refrigerator in a glass container that seals well.

Note: The Rouille will be at its sharpest and most potent right after making and will mellow with age. I recommend letting it sit in the refrigerator for several hours before using.

CHAPTER V

C^{the}o-Conspirator

MY UNCLE JACQUES DIED IN A CAR ACCIDENT, TAKING A TURN TOO FAST AND WRAPPING HIS CAR AROUND A LARGE OLD TREE, A TREE THAT HAD ALREADY KILLED DOZENS OF OTHERS WHO HAD TAKEN THE EXACT SAME TURN AND DIED IN THE EXACT SAME MANNER. It was common knowledge that the tree and corner were haunted, trapping any unsuspecting driver that passed by too quickly.

I first met my Uncle Jacques when I was 8, having returned to France for the third time to discover that my youngest aunt had married a man who was so vibrant others seemed almost dim in comparison. He was so full of life, he compensated for my aunt's feeble hold on reality. He was a big man compared to Pépé, standing maybe 5'9", with wild brown hair and a roguish mustache. If you were looking for a handsome, cool, slightly bad-boy young Frenchman in the late 1960's, well he was it.

When I arrived they had already had their first child, a boy named Eric and had expanded the top floor of the house to make a small single apartment. What I remember most about the apartment was the jaw-dropping view of the Gulf of St. Tropez.

Jacques and I hit it off instantly. He was a house painter and was often busy with his schedule, but not so much that he wouldn't take the time to teach me how to grow tomatoes in the garden, tease me to no end, and treat me not as a child but as a co-conspirator in the game of life. He had a wonderful, infectious smile – and that smile worked on me like a charm.

My grandparent's house had always been full of life before Jacques, but it had been in the form of a quiet, warm welcoming hearth. Now, with Jacques, this was elevated with the addition of spontaneous singing, loud jokes, and a phenomenal garden I helped him tend when I was there. During the summer, the Sunday family lunch now included invited friends and was moved outside, complete with wine, Ricard, paté, mixed green salad, *saucisson sec, Proven-çal* potato salad, cornichons, baguettes, olives, steamed fresh vegetables, pasta with butter, garlic and basil, fresh tomatoes served with homemade mayonnaise, and marinated giant shrimps wrapped in bacon cooked on the barbeque right next to the corn my uncle and I had pinched that morning from a neighbor's field. These meals were always finished off with a massive plate of assorted cheeses and a basket of fruit, washed down with Cognac or some other liqueur we kids smelled but seldom tasted.

After meals the men would play Pétanque, rolling the steel balls across the hard-packed ground at the top of the driveway in front of the empty *Maison de Maître*. Jacques, an exceptional player rivaled only by Pépé, would gladly take me, the youngest and worst player, as his teammate.

While I often helped in the kitchen, Jacques was the first to teach me how to actually cook. There is a difference.

He taught me that the secret to great crêpes was to use beer to thin the batter once the traditional mixture is created. I learned that no matter how well prepared calves brains are, it just couldn't be made edible as far as I was concerned. He taught me the most important thing about cooking: to take joy in preparing a meal, a dish or a dessert, for you will be offering the finished goods up for the pleasure of your family and friends, and their pleasure in something you created is one of the great secret rewards of life.

Once, armed with small stepladders, Uncle Jacques took us to pick almonds off the trees. I had never picked almonds before and discovered that fresh almonds have a fuzzy coat on the shells, and that when you peel off the fur coat and crack the shell, the almond inside is moist and milky. At his enthusiastic insistence, I skeptically tried one and soon was eating them by the handful.

Jacques organized the first and only *méchoui* I ever attended. A *méchoui* is an event where you barbeque a whole lamb, and in preparation Jacques brought home a live young lamb, which he turned loose in the backyard. He told us not to name the lamb, not to play with him too much, and definitely not to get attached as he was for the *méchoui*. We all ignored his advice, naming the lamb in no time (Minou), feeding him incessantly, and playing with him whenever we had time, for the week before the event. Honestly, the thing was fairly stupid, but it was the only lamb I had ever had a chance to play with – and so I became immediately fond of it. Come Sunday, the men got up early and took the now-fattened lamb down to a small lower pasture behind the house, by the stream, near the edge of the forest, in front of the small, old caretaker's cottage. I knew what was to happen in theory, but had never really thought it through to the end. By the time I was up and walked with Stephan to the lower pasture, Minou the lamb was on a spit roasting over the fire pit. It was already golden from the heat and the constant brushing on of the seasoning sauce. In the corner against the stone wall I could glimpse some of its coat and other parts I refused to examine too closely. The smell of the slaughter was still in the air. I was shocked despite all the forewarning. When the rest of the family, and a number of friends, gathered at noon for the feast, I tried eating the roasted lamb meat, but could not, feeling that to do so was somehow to betray my short-lived friendship with Minou. The other children all felt the same, some crying at length over their loss. My uncle had been right in his warnings, but sometimes children can only truly learn a thing for themselves by experience. My grandparent's landlord, Jean-Paul, owner of their house as well as the forever-empty *Maison de Maître*, the vineyards in the front and back of the house, and the surrounding lands, brought out of the old caretaker's cottage a sealed dust-covered bottle over 100 years old and allowed me a sip. It was *vin-de noix* (walnut wine) and honestly tasted like a magical elixir reserved for the gods, thankfully erasing all thought of my spit-roasted friend.

During my fifth trip to France, when I was 11 years old, Uncle Jacques told us to be ready for a very special Sunday outing. From him this was a great portent. Come Sunday, we climbed into his painter's van with our beach towels, masks, snorkel, fins and basic picnic gear and took off. He drove like a wild man, music playing loudly, and going down several narrow back roads before veering off onto a dirt track. After what seemed like half an hour of bouncing and shaking (but was probably no more than 10 minutes), my uncle pulled the van over.

"We're here!"

"Here" was Cap Taillat, a cove then known only to the local fisherman and very few tourists. The cove was sheltered, beautiful, with one small building on the shore. It offered exceptionally clear water with a visibility of at least 50 feet – and no waves at all.

The few others in attendance in an otherwise-deserted stretch of shoreline, were sunbathing in the nude. Not that big a thing, I had seen many topless women at the beach before, but that day while snorkeling and diving down 10 feet or so, I turned and saw an 18-year-old girl swim naked slowly over me on the surface. She was beautiful, and I wanted to look at her, and yet felt I should not look because … and I could not answer the 'because' other than to say possible embarrassment at being seen looking, which made no sense since she was swimming in front of everybody. Little did I know at the time that these conflicting desires were but the beginning and that they, and others of their ilk, were to haunt me, as they haunt every man, for the rest of my life.

A bit before noon, fishing boats started coming in, and we watched as the fishermen, their wives and sons hauled nets and baskets and bottles into the small building on the shore. These were real local fishermen, the men strong, gruff and rough-shaved; the wives were slightly plump but this rested on a frame of strength. Real fisher-men in the South of France, as a general rule, don't mix with tourists, even if they are French tourists. With locals it's a matter of history, as in, is there enough history to warrant trust? Old local men will smoke cigarettes and share a bottle of wine with an old fisherman in a café or play a game of Pétanque in the Place des Lices, but that's because they went to school together as kids, or the local's wife has been buy-ing that fisherman's catch for the last 50 years. In St. Tropez, this mistrust of strangers was further reinforced by the ever-growing tourist trade that impacted and conflicted with the local fisherman's way of life, teasing away sons from the family business with the lure of fast cars, fancy boats and all-night parties. Thus, even back then the traditional fisher-men were a closed lot.

An hour after the last boat finished unloading, my uncle fetched us and brought us to the little building. He was very polite, almost reverent to the fishermen. He turned to me.

"Listen William, what you are about to experience is very special and you are very privileged to be able to attend. This is a traditional fisherman's *Grande Bouillabaisse*. Not like you get in the restaurants, this is not just a soup it is a feast. You see everything here was caught this morning. They only do this once a year."

We went in and were introduced to half-a-dozen fishermen and their families, then were seated. The little house had only one room with a sink, a wood grill that was burning the remains of some driftwood, a couple of shelves, and a long wooden table in the middle made up of thick long boards painted a weathered white. Two long-worn benches ran along the side. I was seated next to my brother, but my uncle, aunt and cousins were far down the table from us. One of the fisherman's wives, a big lady, not pretty but with smiling eyes, sat to my left. Once we got started, she explained each thing we ate as it was served. We had live sea urchins, which I was familiar with as I had collected them when going out sailing with my grandfather, and live sea cucumbers; live small mollusks that contracted when you squeezed lemon on them and that my brother loved; clams steamed in the water of the Mediterranean with herbs; and several varieties of fish that had been cooked over the wood-fired grill. There was more – the table was covered in food, all of it from the sea except for the bread, wine and aioli.

The meal started solemnly with a fisherman's prayer, but in no time voices were raised, along with glasses, in laughter, boasting and toasts. It was a boisterous, joyful feasting, as if we were all one big family – and we were all in on the secret that, for this brief moment, life was meant to be enjoyed to its fullest.

Though I did not like some of what I ate, I heeded my uncle's words, remembering to keep my manners and try everything that was offered. Even at that age, I knew I was being let into the secret world of a slowly disappearing way of life, and I cherished every moment.

On our way home that evening, I thanked my uncle for taking us, telling him how much I had enjoyed it, for I knew that he had pulled many strings to make this happen – I knew because he had said so. He sensed my understanding and gravely nodded before grinning from ear-to-ear and tousling my hair.

A few months after our return to the States, a few months before my parents divorced, Jacques died. I did not cry for him when my mother told me because the place in my heart for him did not seem suddenly empty when he died as it had when I've lost others. It stayed full and has stayed full to this day.

Le Pesto et Le Pistou

The Romans are thought to have introduced basil to northern Italy and Provence. It flourished in both places and became a part of the cooking culture. In northern Italy, they have pesto, and two steps across the border in Provence there is pesto's kissing cousin pistou. The fundamental difference in the two is that pistou does not contain pine nuts or cheese. The following is my recipe for pesto. To make pistou, just leave out the cheese, nuts and chilies and use about 20 percent less olive oil.

While I love them both, and growing up had pistou more often than pesto, personally I prefer pesto. In fact, I am addicted to fresh homemade pesto. Forget the manufactured, preserved concoctions in jars. They compare to fresh homemade pesto like motor oil compares to Normandy butter. Once you've had fresh homemade pesto, not only will you never want to go back to the mass-produced, 12-year shelf-life stuff, you'll also never want to be without a supply of homemade pesto in the fridge.

Purists will tell you that nothing beats pesto made in a large mortar and pestle. I've had it that way, and while the process does have its aesthetic component, it is also very time consuming and requires a lot of effort for a little pesto – and, well, I like a lot of pesto.

In fact, I've gotten into the habit of doubling or tripling the following recipe. Why? Because pesto is good on far more than pizzas and pasta. Put a spoon of fresh pesto on a hot steak just before serving, especially if cooked on an outdoor grill, and discover steak heaven. Mix with homemade mayonnaise for a divine dipping sauce or rub down a chicken in pesto before baking. Make pesto bread (like garlic bread but with pesto) or add it to your scrambled eggs or rice ... endless are the places where fresh homemade pesto can improve your day.

Next time you're at the farmer's market and see that bunch of fresh basil, pick it up, and bring it home. Put on some Paolo Conte and make some fresh pesto. Then enjoy with a friend.

Who knows, you may even become a fresh pesto addict like me. And that's a good thing.

> 1 bunch of fresh basil, preferably sweet Italian basil
> 3/4 cup, approximately, of extra-virgin olive oil
> 4 cloves of garlic, peeled
> 2 small dried peppers, such as bird chilies. (A half a teaspoon of crushed

red chilis will do in a pinch)
1 teaspoon pine nuts
1 teaspoon parmesan cheese
2 pinches of salt

In a food processor, put in peeled garlic cloves, chilies and about 1/3 of the olive oil. Pulse a few times. Add a small handful of basil leaves, but none of the thick stems or twigs. Pulse. Use a wooden spoon between pulses to push leaves down. Add more leaves. Pulse. Add more leaves and another 1/3 of oil. Pulse. Repeat until 3/4 of leaves are used up. Pulse several times until a thick paste is blended, but do not over process to where the leaves are being juiced. Pesto should have texture. Add the rest of the oil and then the rest of the leaves. Add more oil if needed; the exact amount of oil will vary depending on the size of the basil bunch and the size and thickness of leaves. Add salt. Pulse a few times. Add pine nuts and pulse until they are mostly chopped, but not puréed. Now add cheese, but this time just stir cheese in with a spoon.

Place pesto in a glass bowl or jar. Cover and store in the fridge when not being consumed. If kept covered and refridgerated when stored, the pesto will be good for a week or more. I've made jars worth that lasted several weeks.

It will mellow as well, being sharpest immediately after being made.

Note: The above is my basic recipe. You should experiment. There are 100 ways to vary the basic pesto recipe and adjust things to your personal taste. With pesto, if it's good, it isn't wrong. Here are some simple suggestions:

- More garlic if you wish a stronger edge (I usually do).

- Mix in some alternative basil leaves with your sweet basil, such as lemon basil or Thai basil for some exotic blends.

- Skip chilies, for a zero heat experience, or up the amount for a real kick!

- Swap pine nuts with almonds, walnuts or even cashews.

- Try different grated hard cheeses. Some strong cheeses can drastically affect the flavor.

Jacques' Grilled Shrimp Provençal

My uncle made his shrimps using pistou, but it works quite well with pesto, which is how I usually make it. The preparation is quite easy once you have some pistou or pesto sitting around, which is always a good idea.

> 12 large shrimp, shells removed, but tails still on
> 6 slices of good bacon
> 1/4 cup of pesto or pistou
> 4 skewers

Brush pesto quite liberally on both sides of each shrimp (if pesto was in the refrigerator you may need to let it warm up a bit first to liquefy), place them in a bowl, and let marinate in refrigerator for about an hour.

Slice bacon in half. When shrimp are done marinating, wrap a half slice of bacon around the meaty part of shrimp, and then poke your skewer through the center of the shrimp so that the bacon stays in place. Place three shrimps per skewer, leaving a slight gap between each shrimp.

Fire up barbeque to where the coals are graying and hot.

If shrimp were raw to start with, cook shrimp at what would be medium-low heat, fairly high above the coals, and with the lid down to build ambient heat and smoke. You want to cook them slow enough for shrimp to cook through, without bacon becoming too crispy. About a minute before pulling shrimp off, baste them with some more pesto.

If shrimp were pre-cooked, you can place them closer to the fire, as you are effectively just cooking the bacon.

Serve while hot.

CHAPTER VI

le Vieux Port
(The Old Harbor)

THE SIREN FROM *L'USINE* COULD BE HEARD ANY-
WHERE IN OR AROUND ST. TROPEZ, SOUNDING IN
THE MORNING AT 8:00 A.M. TO SIGNAL THE START OF
THE WORKDAY, AT NOON FOR LUNCH, 2:00 P.M. TO
RESTART WORK, AND AGAIN AT 6:00 P.M. TO SIGNAL
THE END OF THE WORK DAY. The church in the center of
town would ring its bell at noon as well, but would wait till
the siren had finished wailing before tolling. Although the
siren was for the workers at *l'Usine*, it set the pace for the
whole town, with shopkeepers closing their doors for lunch
when they heard it go off. You could set your watch by it,
and in fact, most people did, especially in the morning.

When we woke up in the morning, one of the first
things one of us did was to open the red shutters on the
window of our room and let the sun in. It was often decided
by a look, we would eye the shutters, look at each other,
and one of us would nod and do the deed. My grandmother
insisted we close them every night and open them again
every morning, leaving the windows themselves open or

closed depending on the weather. We did this every morning – a small ritual.

My favorite breakfast was a big bowl of Tonimalt, hot milk mixed with several heaping teaspoons of France's answer to Ovaltine, served with a hot, fresh-baked baguette liberally coated in creamy Normandy butter. The only difference between my breakfast and the average working Frenchman's was that I had Tonimalt instead of coffee.

On occasion Mémé would make us soft-boiled eggs. She would serve these in little egg stands that held the egg upright so we could tap around the top with our spoon until we could remove the pointed tip like we were removing a hat. Then we'd scoop out a bit of the egg white, hitting the top of the liquid yolk, and fill the space we'd made with butter, sprinkle some salt, wait till the butter melted, and then stir it all up. Once this was ready, we'd take thin strips of baguette and dip it in, covering the bread with the thick egg-and-butter mixture.

On our fourth trip, we were there in the fall during the grape harvest. Jean-Paul collected up a small group of workers to bring in the grapes from the fields. Stephan and I joined in, more for the experience than the 20 francs we would get paid. We spent the afternoon carrying a basket, walking down the row of vines, and sniping off bunches of grapes. When the basket was full, we would bring it to the large wagon that was gradually filling up. When the wagon was full it was attached to a tractor and taken down the hill to the co-op winery, where it would be weighed, and the grapes tossed into a giant V-shaped pit. At the bottom of the pit, a giant steel screw slowly spun, grabbing the grapes and crushing them. The stems were spit out on the side of the building in large, fruit-fly-infested piles, which, as the season went on, would reach 10-feet tall and whose sweet-pungent alcoholic stench could knock you out if you walked too close. At the end of the day, Jean-Paul opened the *Maison de Maître* and served us all dinner in the grand dining room. Being inside that grand old house was like stepping back in time to before the war, the last time anybody had steadily lived there.

Most of the time we spent in St. Tropez it was summer or close enough that we didn't go to school. If it was Tuesday or Saturday, we would accompany Mémé to the marché to do the grocery shopping. Often, when we were shopping, Mémé would stop at the *patisserie* to pick up a baguette or two, a custard-filled Tarte Tropezienne if we had guests coming, a hard meringue for my brother, and a petit pain au chocolat for me. The *pain au chocolat* was made by wrapping the buttery multi-layered dough of a croissant around a row of bittersweet chocolate squares broken off a large bar. This would be baked, the bar of chocolate inside would melt partially, the dough would puff up, and the whole pastry would be a delicious, buttery, chocolate slice of heaven.

At the Saturday market, the *boucherie chevaline*, the horsemeat butcher, would display his wares out of his traveling butcher shop – and we would sometimes pick up some steaks similar to a flank steak. The horsemeat came from horses specifically bred for their meat, having never been ridden or put to work pulling a cart. Mémé would slow cook these steaks in butter, garlic and fresh-chopped parsley. I grew to love horsemeat beyond beef, but not more than my love for the French boudin noir sausage Mémé would grill for us, along with slow-cooked apples and onions that would caramelize in the pan, and served with mashed potatoes and butter. She always thought it cute that I liked boudin noir, as it was considered health food, something like liver in the States, not a meal children usually liked.

For lunch at the end of our shopping, we would sometimes pick up a Pissaladière, the cold tomato paste and onion pizza that also have anchovies and olives niçoises on them. The first time I had one of these, I protested loudly that it was definitely not a pizza. It was cold and didn't even have melted cheese on it, only to have the vendor inform me that "this is a Pissaladière" and it came before the pizza as I knew it, and anyway pizza still didn't have to have melted cheese or even be hot, and he should know because he was *Provençal*, and pizza was invented in Provence, and that the Italians had stolen the idea to claim it as their own. Any Italian, of course, will tell you that the French are insane on this subject and should be ignored. What I do know was that scholars claim that before there was a France or an Italy, there was Rome, and that Rome's first settled province was the area that is now called Provence, thus the name. And that the first French wine made from grapes (versus honey wine also known as mead) was produced in Provence. So for the people of Provence, who are among other things a mix of French and Italian, to also claim the pizza just may not be that big a stretch.

During the summer, we spent our weekdays either helping around the house (not often), playing in the vineyards or by the creek at the edge of the forest half a kilometer behind the house, or going to the beach.

If we were going to the beach, which we did most often, the routine would go something like this:

Fill a big plastic bottle with iced water and Antesite, an anise-based flavoring, or with sweet mint syrup. Grab a baguette, slice it lengthwise and fill it with pieces of chocolate or Brie, or even better, Caprice des Dieux cheese. Slice some pieces of *saucisson sec*, grab an orange or two, and throw it all in a netted shopping bag. Grab two towels, your mask, fins and snorkel, and throw those in another bag. At that point, we'd head down the hill on the Route Sainte-Anne toward town. Just past the heady wine co-op and before the convent, we would take a left at the fork, walk another two blocks or so, and turn left down the walking path that curved to the right behind the houses and shops – the path providing a shortcut to the coastal road. Once we arrived at the coastal road, we then turned left once again, following the shore till we reached La Plage de la Bouillabaisse. The walk took us about 30 minutes.

This was *our* beach. We swim for hours, go out past the sandy bottom till we snorkeled over the scary, dark seaweed bushes that grow 20 feet below us, lie on the sand, sleep under the sun, and build sandcastles right on the shore break with its tiny six-inch waves. We take breaks for lunch or later make an afternoon snack of the oranges. Then, at 4:00 or 5:00 p.m. we would head back up the hill to Villa St. Joseph, a hot bath, and a home-cooked meal. We did the walk to and from the beach, just the two of us, starting when I was just 6 and my brother 8, safety never being an issue. This was a routine we never tired of. To say we were tan is an understatement.

On rare occasions, after the beach or after school,

usually on Friday or Saturday nights, Pépé would take us to the movies either at the old town theatre or the summer's only outdoor movie theater, which was like a small drive-in but where you walked in, sat on benches, and watched the movie projected on a big screen. The walls around us were nothing more than wood frames with cloth stretched over them, above us only stars. As strange as this was, the first time we went, I completely forgot my surroundings, engrossed in the movie. Pépé would always buy us an ice cream before the movie; he always, invariably, bought a praliné for himself. Pépé loved westerns – and this pretty much decided whether we would go to the movies or not. If a western was screening, we went; if not, we didn't. I remember seeing several Charles Bronson westerns, never noticing beyond the first 30 seconds that all the characters were speaking French.

It was after going to the movies, coming home late at night, driving through the center of town past La Place des Lices, that I first noticed that St. Tropez had the odd habit of having Petanque players come out at 10:00 p.m., 11:00 p.m., even midnight to play in the lit-up town square. The bars around the square would still be open and a mixture of locals and tourists would be out tossing their steel balls, chasing the sweet spot next to the brightly painted, little wooden ball called the cochonet. The late-night games were something I never had a chance to participate in during those years.

The first carnival I ever went to was while living in St. Tropez. Pépé took us, and we had the absolute time of our lives going through the house of horrors, shooting at targets with BB guns, watching the motorcyclist ride round the arena sideways held up by centrifugal force, throwing balls at pyramids of pins, tossing coins onto plates, walking through every corner to be sure we missed nothing. We stayed till we could no longer stand on our feet, clutching tightly our hard-won prizes, a pair of folding metal binoculars, one blue the other red.

On weekends our schedule was first determined by Pépé's bicycle-riding agenda. At least once a month, he would be off riding to some distant destination in Provence, sometimes leaving early Saturday morning and coming back late Sunday night. On weekends when he stayed home, he would either take us sailing or on an exploratory driving adventure to the mountains, the Gorges du Verdon, to visit Roman ruins, local small towns up to the edge of Italy, ancient springs, or some other exotic destination that always had a bit of history and a lesson in it.

Sundays were usually reserved for a big family lunch, so sailing on Sundays often had us leaving at the crack of dawn to be back by noon. The lunches were usually in the backyard, but sometimes we would have family excursions, such as the time we all went up into the Haute-Provence and ate at a restaurant by a lake where Jacques taught me how to fish with my homemade bamboo fishing pole. Later, I used my pole again when we all went for a Sunday picnic by a raging stream, and there I caught my first trout.

Once we went to Fayence to visit my other aunt, and we worked on her overgrown yard in the morning; the first time I ever used a sickle, and then we were sent out to gather wild rosemary, sage and thyme, and finally relaxed with a late lunch in the afternoon.

Many times family and friends would all meet at the beach at La Plage de la Bouillabaisse, and if I got lucky, some adult would pay to rent what I considered at the time a most marvelous contraption, the pédalo, a small two-person boat we powered by pedaling. We would happily pedal around until our legs were ready to fall off, smiling and laughing the whole time.

On very special occasions, such as my grandparent's anniversary, but never more than once during any particular stay in France, on a Sunday night Pépé and Mémé would take us down the hill into town, often with family and friends, for dinner. We would go to a restaurant, not on the tourist-packed, nightclub-filled new harbor but rather at the Vieux Port, the small 2,000-year-old harbor where locals preferred to gather. The owners of the restaurant knew my grandparents and would always come out to greet us all. I would invariably have what to this day is probably my favorite *Provençal* dish, La Soupe de Poisson avec sa Rouille, a Mediterranean fish soup with grated Gruyère cheese, croutons and a strong, garlicky saffron pepper condiment called rouille served on the side. The heady soup would be made fresh from a very select combination of that day's catch and would come out steaming hot in a big porcelain bowl. I would take my croutons and put the rouille on them and drop them into the soup, and then take a big tablespoon full of the cheese and sprinkle it over the top where it would melt in.

La joie de vivre could be summed up in these very special occasions, sitting outside in the oldest part of St. Tropez with its few brightly painted fishing boats pulled up on the beach a dozen feet away, the cool late-summer breeze coming in off the darken bay, dressed in my Sunday best, the sounds of laughter in the air, sharing dinner with my grandparents and brother and aunts and uncles and cousins and friends.

Un Bon Boudin Noir

Boudin Noir can be tricky to find in the States, but it is out there. Fabrique Delice out of Northern California makes them, sold in packs of four, and available at a number of specialty markets. Though related, French Boudin Noir is not the same as the German variant, or English "black pudding," or even the Italian, though I must say I have had an Italian version that had raisins and pine nuts in it that was quite good. The French version has its own mix of spices, onions and parts of pig. As is the custom in France, every *Charcuterie* will have its own exact recipe.

In case you were wondering, Boudin Noir is very different from Boudin Blanc; they cannot be substituted. And Cajun Boudin is also a totally different sausage.

At Mémé's house, Boudin Noir was considered health food, in large part because of its high iron content. I've had people refuse to try it because it is made with blood -- pig's or cow's blood depending on the region. I've also convinced a few of these naysayers to try it and created enthusiastic converts.

Lastly, yes, there's a fair bit of butter involved in this recipe, but I promise it is worth it.

4 Boudin Noir sausages
2 fresh apples
1 large yellow onion
4 tablespoons butter

Core, quarter and slice the apples, leaving skin on. Halve onion, slice it, and then cut the slices in half.

Place 2 tablespoons of butter in a large skillet at medium heat. As soon as the butter melts, toss in apples and onions and stir so apples and onions are well mixed together and coated with butter. Let them cook for a good eight minutes, stirring occasionally.

Pinprick each sausage three or four times along one side to help keep them from bursting. After eight minutes, add sausages to skillet along with 1 tablespoon of butter and lower heat to medium-low.

Stir apples and onions every couple of minutes so that they brown and caramelize all over. Flip Boudin Noir when it is well-grilled, usually after about 10 minutes. When you flip Boudin Noir, add last tablespoon of butter.

The Boudin Noir will release some juices. Make sure you mix these into caramelizing apples and onions.

When the sausages are grilled on both sides, remove and serve along with sautéed caramelized apples and onion mixture.

Note: This dish is often served with mashed potatoes, making for a very hearty meal. I find that if you just add a salad, such as the Salade Campagnarde given earlier it is enough.

CHAPTER VII

the Gift

I HAD GOOD FRIENDS IN FRANCE. When Stephan went up to the Alps to go skiing with his school, the girls of the same grades from the alternate school also went. They didn't mix except for on the slopes, which is where my brother met a very nice and intelligent girl named Marie, who, as fate would have it, was Pierre's oldest sister. Between Pierre and Marie, there was Chantal, and the five of us made up The Gang. Other kids would move in and out, but the five of us were the solid core, and we hung out together every chance we had.

Their parents owned the film-processing shop right on the new harbor, tucked in amongst the cafés, clubs and gift shops, across from the million-dollar yachts and sailing boats, dwarfing the outnumbered local fishing fleet. In the summer, the store was always packed; their father working long hours in the tourist season to make enough money to hold them through the quiet winters.

Our friends' parents were part of that small select group of amazing young couples that would always make time for you regardless of your age, always treated you with intelligence, love and kindness, and thus, had absolutely great kids. If the world had more parents like these two, there is no doubt it would be a much better place.

Once in a while, their mother, a tall, thin, curly-haired beautiful woman who had a sense of that sophisti-cated French graciousness and nobleness and yet was quick to smile and full of warmth and compassion, would take The Gang out on excursions. On our first trip together, shortly after we all first met, she took us in her base model Citroen station wagon, not the famed DS wagon, but rather some-thing slightly better than a 2CV, and we drove to Monaco and toured the Cousteau Museum. Afterward, sitting on the steps of this big, beautiful, white palace of a museum on the bluffs above the Mediterranean, the sea spread out before us, as we ate ice cream bars, tired from the day yet laughing at the absolute magic of it all, at that moment, despite our young ages, a bond of love was formed.

Whenever we were in St. Tropez during the sum-mer, we would stop at their apartment on our way to the beach and pick up Marie, Chantal and Pierre so we could all head out together. Sometimes we would never make it out of the apartment, getting caught up in books, discus-sions, various games, especially the French version of the card game Hearts, which on occasion we would play late into the night, after a quick call to Mémé for permission.

When not at the beach, The Gang would wander around St. Tropez, stopping at their parents shop just off the new harbor just to say, "Hi." We would run through the windy streets playing tag, work our way up to the citadel, or play in the vineyards on the outskirts of town. We even went so far as to walked out to La Plage des Cannebiers, which, while only about three or four kilometers, felt like a long walk when you're unfamiliar with the road and young. I remember coming back late that afternoon, barely able to walk, so thoroughly exhausted from all the swimming and running around we had done that day.

Once, their enchanting mother took us all out to gather *Pignons de Provence*, the pine nuts that are produced by the low-altitude pine trees in the area. We went to a particular grove of pine trees she knew and, being the best climbers, Chantal and I climbed the trees, tossing the pine-nut-rich cones down for everybody to gather. I had never known pine nuts to even exist before this – that pinecones actually had nuts you could eat growing inside of them was to me, at that age, another of God's marvelous inventions. And not just a few; if you got lucky, a big cone could net you two-dozen nuts! I had picked up many a pinecone in the States and not once did I ever see a pine nut in them. By the time we finished harvesting the cones, I was tired, my muscles ached, and I was covered in resin and scratches, but was so praised by my friend's mother for the good job I had done that all complaints vanished, the sticky patches of sap now badges of honor.

Pierre had a collection of the Asterix et Obelix comic books. These French comic books, despite being thin, all had hard covers and were printed in much higher quality than American comics. We would sit together and read them; I would sound out the French words and ask him to define the ones I didn't know. With the help of Pierre, Asterix and Obelix I learned to read French, at least to the comic book level, and I developed a life-long love for France's two greatest defenders against the Romans.

Pépé brought Marie, Chantal and Pierre along on a few of our weekend excursions. The most memorable being when he took us up to the mountains to the first snow of the season. In a meadow in the middle of nowhere, we built our snow forts. We built huge forts with four-foot high walls, and ammo shelves loaded with snowballs, and windows carved out so we could keep an eye on the enemy. We ended the day at dusk tired, wet, cold and "loving life."

Most of all, we went to the beach together. We swam together. We built sandcastles together. We shared our lunches and drinks and chocolates and snacks.

The Gang's pecking order had Marie, the oldest, with soft, curly, reddish-brown hair, a sprinkling of freckles, kind eyes, generally easygoing manner and a disarming smile, sharing the leadership mantel with Stephan. She was followed by Chantal, who had straight, dark-brown hair, piercing eyes, was thinner, tougher, a little bit tomboy and, when not angry at the world, displayed an almost empathic understanding of people, or maybe just me. Her tough edge meant she didn't always like to do what her older sister said. In the pecking order she was tied with me, who was just slightly younger and was known to object to my own brother's rule at times. Bringing up the rear was Pierre as the youngest – and always the wildest and most energetic of the bunch. Pierre and I did share a special bond though, formed those first days in school, and we often had our heads together creating mischief.

We started up The Gang when I was six, and we hung out with each other whenever we came to France, which was for several months usually every year or two.

At first, it was Marie and my brother and Pierre and I, with Chantal the odd man out. As we grew older, Chantal and I built up a stronger bond, but Pierre was always my best friend.

I say the bonds between girls and boys grew stronger, but it was into that unknown territory. With us so young there was just a hint of what could be someday, with that someday moving closer all of the time; this hint really showing up most with the oldest two, especially on that last summer when The Gang was together.

On that trip, my brother was 13 and Marie 14, and though they never kissed or anything, at least in front of me, it was obvious there was a bond beyond what we all generally felt for each other. I was only eleven years old, and Chantal and I had a tenuous and mysterious emotion growing stronger between us as that summer passed. I knew there was something – and I knew it was there because she was a girl, and though I loved Marie like an older sister and Pierre as my best friend, my love for Chantal was flavored with that something else. She was, without my even knowing it, my first love.

I remember late during our last summer together, Pierre realized during an outing around town that something was going on because I was paying more attention to Chantal than him. He had a hysterical fit, demanding that I stop talking to Chantal … period. It was one of those unreasonable demands that a 10-year-old can make and really mean. I refused, explaining the illogic of what he asked, and he sulked for the rest of the afternoon. Fortunately, it didn't last. He came to his senses – and The Gang stayed intact until the end of summer.

Years later, shortly after I was married, on my first return trip to France since my teen years, my brother, my new wife Tiaré and I, met up with Chantal and Marie, along with Marie's husband and child at their home in Bordeaux. Unfortunately, Pierre couldn't make it. Chantal was still single. After the first 10 minutes of awkwardness, we found our old comfortable relationship, slipping into our friendship like a long lost, but comfortably worn, pair of slippers, and had a wonderful night. Yet, I had a most unusual experience that night. Looking at Chantal, looking in her eyes, I felt as if I had somewhere lost a life – a life unlived but oh so close you could taste it, where Chantal and I had reunited as young adults, lived together, and shared many wonderful experiences. A life that could have been, had things been slightly different – a feeling of loss for something that would never be. All this while still having no regrets about the life I now led.

I realized something else; that people we love in childhood, we love forever. Not in the sense that we would love them today, decades later, if we met them by chance. They are different people now, sometimes unrecognizable to us; but rather that we will always love who they were then; what they meant to us then. That time, that place, that little universe lives forever in our hearts, outside the stream of time.

You see, that last summer we were all together in St. Tropez as kids, we spent as much time together as we could. It was as if we knew something soon would be lost, without knowing what it was. I can tell you now it was innocence.

The very last time The Gang went to the beach together was also the very last time we were ever all together as kids. We all knew we wouldn't be seeing each other again for a while, but none of us knew for just how long. It was the end of summer and my brother and I were going back to the States the next day and try as we might we couldn't stop time. The day went forward all too quickly into afternoon, and then early evening – and the time came when we all had to go home. My brother and I would take our walk through St. Tropez, climbing the hill back to Villa St. Joseph for the last time. As we prepared to leave the beach, we all changed out of our bathing suits while wrapped in big towels. I changed, packed the last of our stuff, and waited for the others to finish. Our friends' mother was already there to pick them up and everybody was melancholy. As I waited, heart heavy, Chantal was standing about eight feet away wrapped up in her giant beach towel changing out of her bathing suit. She took the last of her bathing suit off, kicked it into a pile then turned to face me and opened up her towel, just a brief glimpse, gave me a quick smile and closed it up again, turned away, and finished getting dressed.

This was the last childhood memory I had of Chantal, and at the time I didn't realize what a great gift it was. It was later, when I was mature enough to look back and understand, that I realized she had given me in that brief moment the greatest parting gift she could offer.

Lemon & Olive Chicken with French Green Beans

I love this dish. I make it often for family and friends. Its roots are firmly planted in Mémé's kitchen, and it brings me pleasure every time I make it for somebody new, and they like it or love it. There's nothing like cooking a meal for a friend and watching his or her face light up when they are served or stutter in absolute delight while eating or asking for thirds.

This recipe is one that makes allowances for changes by a savvy cook. First try it as suggested, and then make it your own.

    1 large roasting chicken
4 sweet Italian sausages
3 ounces of salt pork or thick cut pancetta
2 1/2 cups of dry white wine
1 1/2 pounds of fresh French green beans – the long thin kind.
1 large yellow onion
1 lemon
4 small fresh, sweet red peppers
6 garlic cloves
12 black oil-cured olives
2 tablespoons of pine nuts
1 heaping tablespoon of *Herbes de Provence*
1/2 teaspoon of fresh ground cumin

1/4 teaspoon cayenne
1 ounce pastis, preferably Ricard brand.
Mediterranean sea salt

Preheat oven to 400 degrees.

Place chicken in a large Dutch oven, ideally a large Creuset model.

Cut lemon in half, cut a 1/4-inch slice from each face and reserve. Squeeze juice from two halves over chicken, making sure to coat as much of chicken as possible. Take one of squeezed-out lemon halves and stuff it into chicken cavity. If chicken came with gizzards, place these in Dutch oven outside chicken. Let chicken sit with its lemon-juice coating while preparing the rest of ingredients.

Take green beans and one at a time trim the very ends off both ends, easily done by hand by just snapping the very tips off. Place trimmed beans into a large bowl. When you've trimmed all the beans fill bowl with water and let beans sit.

Chop onion into 1/2-inch pieces and set aside.

Slice sweet peppers in half, scrape and discard seeds, then slice the halves again lengthwise, and reserve.

Slice sausages into 2-inch lengths and reserve.

Chop salt pork or pancetta into 1/2-inch cubes and reserve.

Return to chicken and rub the *Herbes de Provence* onto chicken, coating entire chicken, top to bottom, letting any excess fall into Dutch oven.

Position chicken in Dutch oven breasts up.

Dust chicken with ground cumin.

Take half of green beans let them drip dry before placing them around chicken, pushing them to the bottom, but not under chicken.

Take chopped onions and sprinkle them over green beans.

Take sliced peppers and distribute them evenly around chicken onto green beans.

Take salt-pork pieces and distribute evenly around chicken onto green beans and stuff two or three pieces into chicken.

Take remaining green beans and after letting them drip dry, surround chicken with them, covering the previous green beans, onions, peppers and salt pork.

Cut each garlic clove into 4 pieces and sprinkle onto green beans.

Place cut sausages evenly around chicken on top of green beans.

Sprinkle pine nuts evenly around chicken over green beans.

Spread olives around chicken, over green beans, while also stuffing two olives into chicken.

Pour 2 1/2 cups of wine around chicken, over green beans but not over chicken.

Pour ounce of pastis around chicken, over green beans but not over chicken.

Dust green beans with cayenne.

Place reserved lemon slices over meatiest part of chicken breasts, one on each side.

Lightly salt chicken and lemon slices with Mediterranean sea salt.

Put lid on and stick it in oven on middle shelf or as high as Dutch oven lid will allow it to go and still clear.

Cook for two hours at 400 degrees.

After one hour, take the lid off and be careful to let hot steam vent away from you, and with a long wooden spoon stir up green beans just a bit. If most of liquid has evaporated (it can happen if the lid has large gaps – but usually doesn't), add 1/2 cup of water and 1/2 cup of white wine. Put the lid back on, and back into the oven she goes.

At the end of second hour, take the lid off, and be careful to let hot vapors escape away from you.

Serve directly from Dutch oven, as

chicken will be too delicate to move. Cut pieces off chicken (it should be practically falling apart) and serve with big spoonfuls of green beans along with all the rest that has acquainted itself well.

You can choose from a number of different accompaniments for this dish. I suggest oven-roasted rosemary potatoes (cut potatoes into 1-inch cubes, toss with minced rosemary, olive oil and sea salt, spread on a cooking platter and roast 45 minutes at 400 degrees, mixing occasionally). Or delicious with orzo pasta – just ladle juices from chicken over cooked pasta.

You should also serve some warm baguettes, as people will want to mop up every drop.

Mangez lentement, riez, et savourez la belle vie. (Eat slowly, laugh and savor the good life.)

CHAPTER VIII

*the*Last Trip

*I*HAD A VERY DIFFICULT TIME WRITING ABOUT THIS LAST TRIP. I didn't want it to be about my parent's bitter divorce, custody battles, my brother and I fighting with my mother, or about my father's sickness, yet these things all happened in the almost four years between voyages and contributed to a greatly changed perspective on the last childhood trip.

The circumstances that led to this trip were all unpleasant, not that I wasn't eager to return to France, but rather all the orbiting family chaos was contributing to the end of my childhood far too prematurely. The situation was made all the worse by my father being in the hospital when we left.

So I will skip the events leading to this trip, the last trip to France during my childhood. A trip made when I was 14, and for reasons that the fates alone could explain would not happen again for another 14 years.

We flew to London and proceeded to take the train to South Hampton, where we boarded an overnight ferry that took us to Le Havre. Do not rest your head on the window of a train in England, for the shockwave of an oncoming train passing what seems to be mere inches away at 80 miles per hour is enough to not only bruise your head, but the suddenness of it can strain your heart.

The ferry was uneventful, except for that momentous moment when we crossed out of English waters into French territory, and I was finally able to order a beer. At 14, a time when it felt like life, my parents and even my brother were always telling me what to do, having the power to order a beer mattered greatly.

My mother had not driven a stick-shift in a dozen years and proceeded to stall our rental car mid-intersection as we left the rental agency. Not a simple stall but that bucking-bronco type of stall where the car jerks back and forth several times, and then dies. She would restart the car and get back on the horse, so to speak, for another few yards. I didn't know whether to laugh or cry as the drivers of the cars around us honked and screamed obscenities, so I did both. I ended up just laying down on the backseat out of sheer embarrassment until we eventually made it out of the intersection.

The misadventures continued with the car's electrical system dying within an hour of leaving the lot. I knew the omens had been revealed and feared what we were in for.

We made our way to Mont St. Michel. This was my first time visiting, unless one believes in past lives at which point I can truly say this was definitely not my first time. Since many don't believe in reincarnation, let's just say, for congeniality's sake, that it was my first time.

As we approached, the island was shrouded and, as if nature were playing a magic trick using the fog and mists, it started to peek through, slowly building into reality. Mont St. Michel is a massive rock outcropping in a large flat bay. Atop this outcropping is a magnificent cathedral, built-up over hundreds of years, but all of it dating from before our great, great grandparent's were a gleam in their parent's eyes. Surrounding the cathedral is a town with streets far too narrow for cars, which are not allowed on the island, and around the town are ramparts that tower over the bay. The tides are such that when they are out, the island is surrounded by sand, and when fully in it is surrounded by eight to 10 feet of water. The story goes that the tide can come rushing in faster than a horse can run, and this is true, but only at the perfect alignments of sun and moon. Still, the Mont St. Michel, due to its natural defenses stood against many an invader for centuries. The island is no longer truly an island today as a raised earthen road has been built to it – and this exemplifies the modern contradiction of the place. It is magical and mystical – and its history is wild and glorious. All of that is there to see and feel when you walk its streets, gaze out over the ramparts, and enter the cathedral, but also there to be seen and felt are two-dozen tour buses, crowds of camera-toting tourists, and enough souvenir vendors to compete with Disneyland. Past and present collide, and while tarnishing this mystical place, they do not come near to ruining it. The spirit of Mont St. Michel still abounds, as if the rocks of the ramparts, or the bedrock of the island itself were the source.

My mother had become a real estate agent after the divorce and had visions of doing what she called "interna-

tional real estate," which consisted of selling French properties to wealthy Americans. With that in mind, we drove on
to visit and spend the night at the home of a potential client,
in a chateau in the countryside on the outskirts of Bordeaux.
We arrived in the middle of a hot day. I had a miserable
headache and Stephan had a severe nosebleed, the first of
several on this trip. I was ushered to a high-ceiling private
room on the second floor, the bed so high I needed steps
to get in. Head pounding, I climbed into this antique bed
with pillows and comforters loaned from heaven, in this
Bordeaux chateau, and thankfully, quickly passed out.

When I awoke, it was late afternoon, the crickets
were singing outside, the sun shined golden, and the hushed
murmurs of voices could be heard downstairs. I dressed
feeling strangely at "Home" and descended to meet our
hostess. Home with a capital H is not a place or a thing, but
rather an aesthetic. We each have our own version of Home
that lives close to the soul. Many little details, nuances,
and wisps of dreams go into defining it. You can make a
Home for yourself by creating a place that has enough bits
of art and magic to approximate your ideal, or sometimes,
on those rare occasions, you step into a place that parallels
enough of your own sense of beauty and *divine livingness*
that it's felt down deep.

Our hostess was a woman in her seventies. I only
knew her as Madame. Her husband had died and to avoid
loneliness she had invited a half dozen of her widowed
friends to come live at the chateau with her. Madame was
charm and grace and nobility, all belonging to a lost world.

The chateau was U-shaped, with the main building
in the center; the two arms housing the servants' quarters

on one side; and the stables on the other, reaching out down a slight incline, overlooking gentle rolling hills of the countryside of Bordeaux. The drive came up the center and made a circle around the ancient fountain in front of the main house. It was in need of repair here and there, but the main house was still fully functional and decorated in a subdued Louis XIV. The manicured gardens were not quite as manicured or anywhere as large as Versailles, but enough majesty and romance remained in the chateau and the grounds to enthrall. A spiral stone staircase leading down from the ground floor was locked with a steel gate. When I inquired, Madame, the Lady of the house, said, "That goes down to the dungeons. It's not safe for you to go down there." I stood at those gates and stared down for a good five minutes, letting my imagination go wild. After an early dinner, Stephan and I took a walk around the property. It took us about an hour, as the grounds must have been over 100 acres, mostly forest. When my mother told me the woman was selling her wonderful stately home for only $340,000, I nearly cried.

Madame died in her chateaux before it was sold.

The next day, my mother was to visit other homes for sale in the area. She dropped us off with a young couple, some friends of hers, to await her return. We were a bit uncomfortable at being suddenly dropped on some strangers out in the middle of the countryside, but that discomfort was soon remedied with style, grace and good taste when they brought out a giant bowl of fresh-picked strawberries along with an overflowing ceramic pot of homemade *Crème Chantilly*. We four sat at the table in their garden eating and laughing till both bowls were empty. They were the best strawberries I have ever eaten.

While on the road, we would stop at small inns for the night. On these evenings, we often argued with my mother about how the windows in the rooms of the inns should be managed. She would open them wide as soon as we arrived and turn on all the lights. The windows would then stay open all night. Since the windows were wide open, with lights on, we invariably had a room full of mosquitoes to contend with. To her it was nothing – to me they sounded like German Messerschmitts on strafing runs as I tried to sleep. I would often stay up for hours, swatting invisible mosquitoes in the dark.

While working our way from Bordeaux to St. Tropez, I spent a night, a miserable, miserable night, dodging and swatting in a tiny family-run inn with only two rooms above the bar / café in a six-building crossroads town. I had a few hours sleep and a half-dozen new mosquito bites to show for the night. In the morning, we went downstairs where there were only three tables in the café in addition to the bar. One table was occupied, and it held the owner-bartender father and his children. The mother came out of the kitchen with a *Terrine de Campagne* she had just pulled out of the oven, and she gave us a big slice before serving her husband and children. To me, the steaming *terrine* filled with meats and spices was about as good as it could get. Our hostess noticed my pleasure. With a big smile, she gave me an extra slice to go as we headed out. I sat in the backseat of our little car – I was relegated to the backseat the whole trip – and nibbled happily on my slice, savoring every morsel. My mother told me not to eat it all in one sitting. I ignored her, refusing to let her spoil my one pleasure derived from that family-run inn.

The next day in the Périgord, we feasted on a variety of patés and foies gras surrounded by some of the oldest cave paintings known to man. I have since learned that these paintings are no longer available for public view as the traffic of bodies in those caves was accelerating their deterioration.

We stopped at the Gouffre de Padirac, a little-known natural phenomenon that is guaranteed to enthrall anyone who still has a child buried somewhere in their hearts. In the middle of the countryside, at a small building, we purchased tickets and walked over to a large sinkhole in the ground. The hole drops down about 200 feet. We descended the stairs to the bottom of this abyss, entered a side cave, and walked ever downward along the path until we came to a small dock on an underground river. We boarded our small-flat-bottom tin boat and floated downstream; dimly lit by a wire strung with simple light bulbs, led by our guide who would occasionally use his long pole to ensure we went in the right direction. The ride eventually ended in a massive series of caves and a lake where the river disappears down a whirlpool. The site operators would take a picture of each boat full of passengers and sell it at the store above ground. We bought a picture of us all in the boat, and my brother and I kept it for years, even after it had turned sepia from age.

The road trip ended with a short stay in St. Tropez. We were ecstatic to see our grandparents and marveled at how they seem to not have changed at all in the intervening four years, while for us a lifetime had passed.

The stay in St. Tropez was filled with mixed emotions and melancholy moments. No, my mother was not getting remarried; the gentleman had changed his plans. Yes, we would go sailing with Pépé. No, Marie, Chantal and Pierre were not in town – the whole family had left on vacation and so we would not be seeing them – a crushing blow.

This stay in St. Tropez is my least memorable. The hill behind the house, past the vineyards, across our old stream, that had been wild forestlands, was now sporting condominiums, the stream having been partially buried.

My brother and I walked around town, down our old favorite paths to the beach, the old harbor, the creek and through the vineyards, but we wandered like lost souls in search of something solid we could inhabit.

The whole time I tried to grab hold of the magic and hang on, for I knew it was there.

It wasn't easy.

I did capture enough to sustain life for another 14 years.

Les Vins de Provence

Provence has been making wine since before Caesar's time, and in fact, vines existed in the Provence region 600 years before even the Greeks arrived. To say that Provence has a history of winemaking is an understatement. No place in France has a longer history.

Provence is loosely defined by: the Italian border on the east, the western edge of the Rhone valley to the west, the upper edge of the Alpes de Haute Provence and the northern border of Drome to the north, and the Mediterranean Sea to the south. Within this broad area there are over 1,250 wineries and dozens of appellations. I have not tasted every appellation in the greater Provence area – much less wine from all 1,250 wineries, but that doesn't keep me from having an opinion or two to share.

In France, wine is less about specifically which grape or combination of grapes it is made from, though that does play a significant role especially if you are the winemaker, but for the drinker rather it is more about where it is made. Wines are named by region, the appellation usually being the name of the place, defining exactly where the grapes must be grown to be considered, but often leaving to the individual winery the exact proportions of the varieties to be blended. Some wine appellation regions are tiny, nothing more than a few dozen acres. Place is incredibly significant. It is the soil, sun, wind and history of the place.

It is the *terroir*.

After that it gets personal.

Here is the thing: A huge part of the joy of wine, at least in my view, is having a sense of place that goes with the wine. Wine is more than the taste on the palate; it is place, memories, history and art. This is why with wine, taste is such a personal thing – it includes one's romantic notions.

Thus, the following comments on just a few of the many types of wines found in Provence are highly affected by my own romantic notions.

A broad comment about Rosé

Rosé is the wine of Provence. One should only drink it well chilled on hot days. It is best shared amongst friends. Rosé is not something one collects; it is something one drinks. A good *Provençal* rosé that has been well chilled, served on a hot day, and shared amongst friends, will eliminate any reservations you may ever have formed about drinking rosé.

Côtes de Provence

This appellation includes the rosé of St. Tropez I grew up with. My disenchantment of what has happened to the St Tropez of my childhood is reflected in my lukewarm feelings about the current *rosé* from St Tropez. It is a wine that has sold out; it has lost its magic. In general, my experience with the rest of the Côtes de Provence wines has been very much hit and misses. I must admit the hits did include some wonderful rosés.

Tavel

The Tavel appellation only makes rosé, and they do a darn fine job of it. I have never had a bad Tavel. It is always clean, crisp, dry yet with various levels of fruitiness and floral bouquet. Never had a bad Tavel that bears remembering.

Beaumes de Venise

A named villages classification of the Côtes du Rhone appellation, Beaumes de Venise is best known for their sweet dessert wine Muscat de Beaumes de Venise. When I was a child I would on occasion get a shot glass of Muscat de Beaumes de Venise as a treat from my grandfather. At its worst, it is good. At its best it is reminiscent of the golden nectar of the gods handed down from Mt. Olympus.

The best I've ever had was when we had a small bottle after dinner at the best pizzeria in the world. Let me digress for a moment and explain. In late December 2007, we stopped for the night at a wonderful inn that had been in the same family for generations. The inn was located in the old part of Vaison La Romaine, that is to say across the old Roman bridge and up the hill, just under the ruins of the castle. At the inn, we asked for dinner recommendations, and the owner suggested a pizza place just walking distance down the narrow cobblestone road. She mentioned there might be a wait. We'd been in France for weeks and there had never been a wait anywhere, usually the opposite in the dead of winter. Well, there was a wait, and when we finally were seated and ate the pizza that came, all was revealed. It was, by far, the best pizza I have ever eaten at a restaurant. Ever. And to put a cap on it they brought us a small bottle of Muscat de Beaumes de Venise that poured out like liquid gold. When I asked the owner where it came from and how could I buy some, he shrugged and said a buddy of his had a small winery in Beaumes de Venise – and if I stuck around to the second week of January I could go pick some up. Alas, we had to be in Paris the next day …

I want to mention that Beaumes de Venise also makes a very friendly red; my favorite coming from Château Redortier. It is one of those slightly fruity Rhone reds where you can taste the hot sun on the grapes and feel the wild rosemary and thyme from the nearby mountains, all without the hard edge you sometimes find in Côtes du Rhones.

Bandol

I have not had the pleasure of as many tastes of Bandol red as I would like. I've had a half-dozen fair-to-good bottles, and a few fantastic ones that had a depth and complexity that warranted further exploration – much further exploration.

I have had my share of Bandol rosé and must say they have always been good.

Côtes du Luberon

This is the appellation that covers the
Luberon Valley. You very rarely see any
Côtes du Luberon wines in the States.
Supposedly this is because they are
"simple wines with little complexity."
Well, after sharing a bottle with my wife,
sitting in the car eating caillettes for lunch
on a rainy day, watching the emerald
green yet crystal clear river flow by in the
beautiful town of Fontaine de Vaucluse, I
formulated my own hypothesis: The wine
is so friendly and easy-to-drink, that none
of it ever manages to leave the region.

Côtes de Ventoux

This appellation, north of the Luberon
Valley, is supposed to have some
wonderful wines. I'm sure they exist,
positive they are out there, but I have yet
to find one. Clearly more exploration is
warranted.

Les Baux de Provence

Let me tell you a little story. South of Avignon, there's this wonderful little town called St Remy de Provence, where Nostradamus was born and where there's a great restaurant, well more than one, but our favorite was the Bistro des Alpilles, but that story is for another time. The thing is, if you head east out of town on the D99 and look very carefully on the right you'll see a tiny little sign for a one-lane road called Chemin de Romanin and a place called Château Romanin. Take a right on this little road.

Keep going through the trees, past the glider field, the vineyards and *Provençal garigue*, following those tiny little signs that say Château Romanin. Eventually the road dead-ends at the base of the starkly beautiful mountains known as Les Alpilles.

On your right, sitting at the top of an out-thrust of the mountain are the ruins of a 1,000-year-old castle, the original Château Romanin that was built on a site that was known to be special before Christ was born. To your left will be the slightly disconcerting and just a wee bit mythical site of two huge doors built into the side of a mountain. This is the new Château Romanin.

Underground.

The new Château Romanin was built with the intent to take advantage of the naturally cooling properties of being under a mountain to make and store wine. And it works ... quite well actually.

Château Romanin is a biodynamic winery. That means they are not only organic, but also work to be in harmony with the Earth, harvest by phases of the moon, pick by hand, and a host of other somewhat esoteric practices. It's a bit complicated, but quite romantic and somehow very appropriate to wine – especially good wine.

Château Romanin is so good at making biodynamic wine that not that long ago they won a gold medal for best biodynamic wine in France. They've also been on a number of "best-of" lists, including best small wineries of France, best rosé and best reds of Provence, and the like.

The real treat is to tour the winery and visit *La Cathèdrale*, built deep into the mountain this underground storage area is filled with giant wood barrels, 30-foot arching columns and carved pillars, raw stone walls, and appropriate mood lighting. Imagine if a crew of Dwarves from *Lord of the Rings* had decided to build a majestic winery under a mountain, a veritable underground cathedral dedicated to

Bacchus. It looks quite a bit like that. It is frankly awe-inspiring.

What makes it all better is that much of the wine is really good. Their *rosé* is a giant step above the norm. Delightfully complex for a *rosé*, crisp and clean, and it somehow raises your spirit at each sip. And their other selections are worth tasting, knowing the odds are you will find at least one or two "must haves," especially their gold-winning *Cœur* wine, possibly the best Baux de Provence wine I've ever had.

Château Romanin does not disappoint in helping establish a unique sense of place, inspired memories and a wonderful injection of art into life. I still have a few dust-covered bottles that I just look at and remember. One of them is the *Cœur* from the year they won best in France. Someday, I will actually open them up and drink them, but it will have to be a very special occasion.

Château Romanin also makes its own small production of biodynamic olive oil from olive trees on the estate. I'm told it's really good. It must be, they have been sold out every time I go. Apparently as soon as the word goes out that they are pressing and bottling the oil, people from all over come and buy a few bottles, or a case or more, and within a month of the pressing it is all gone, until the next year.

They also make their own honey. They keep several hives on the estate so as to keep the biodynamics of pollination working or something like that. They harvest and sell a limited supply of two types of biodynamic honey: wildflower and forest honey. The wildflower is good. The forest honey is sensational. When is the last time you had honey you thought was sensational?

So, the next time you are traveling along the D99 just east of St Remy de Provence, look for the little sign on the side of the road and follow it to Bacchus' magical underground cathedral. See if you don't develop a few of your own romantic notions.

EPILOGUE

the Bolthole

I AWOKE TO THE SMELL OF COFFEE DRIFTING UP FROM THE KITCHEN. The sun's rays were streaming in through the window, which meant that it was at least 11:00 a.m., as the building across the street would block the sun any earlier in the morning.

I could hear ambient sounds of the street below. It was a narrow medieval passage that trucks avoid at all cost, and only the local residents' cars ever wandered through, which meant the sounds you heard were of passing conversations, laughing children, clacking of high-heeled shoes, and slapping of sandals on the cobblestone road. Our village house had been built in the 16th century, and the sounds outside my window hadn't changed for the last 500 years.

I threw on my favorite white linen lounge-around pants and shirt and wandered downstairs. My wife looked up as I entered the kitchen.

"Hi. I got some croissants from Madeleine's and some homemade jam from Madame Toti. I'm not sure what kind of berry it is, but it smells good."

Madeleine's was the bakery down the street where my wife had not only become fast friends with the young woman running it, but was threatening to become a fixture in the back as she learned the secrets of baking French breads and pastries. In return my wife, who had grown up in Hawaii, had shown Madeleine how to make Hawaiian popovers, causing quite a stir in the neighborhood.

As for Madame Toti, she was an old woman several doors down who, despite the language barrier, had adopted my wife. She would lecture to her in heavily accented *Provençal* French at length about the ways of the world circa 1950, pat her on the hand, and then give her something out of her astounding roof garden.

After breakfast, I sat in front of the village house strumming mindlessly on the ukulele, watching the foot traffic go by. I had had a very productive night of writing and needed to recharge my batteries. It seemed that I was often doing my best writing when we came to this bolthole of ours. Its uncomplicated simplicity and beauty, combined with the small French village lifestyle we led while here, instilled a *joie de vivre* that opened up enough space in my private universe to unleash my muse.

Returning to France had given me back, in large part, what I had thought lost. Not innocence, though it did allow me to see the innocence lost, but returning gave me what I can best express as the reduction of the cynicism that modern life so easily instills.

In France, for some odd reason, we, as does most everybody else, gleefully try to turn meals into works of art. We take walks, hang out at cafés, or explore the never-ending list of small towns where one can just let history seep into your bones. We visit the unlimited supply of wineries and distilleries, or farms making cheeses, saucisons, patés, or selling something fresh that you just can't get in a store.

And let's not even begin to get started on the myriad restaurants.

Simply put the food, wine, sun and the air itself, all just smell, taste and feel better.

For now, in France, outside her big cities, life is still lived in pursuit of its joys.

Magic truly is in the air.

When I return to the States, as I have to do, to work and pursue my career, it is as if I'm holding my breath, gradually using up the stored magic, waiting for the day when it can be replenished.

But for this trip, while at our bolthole, I could sit on the 1,000-year-old front step, soak up some magic, and happily pretend I know how to play the ukulele.

That is until my wife stepped out of the house. She had her blue-Hawaiian-print-canvas-shopping bag in hand.

"It's Thursday, I'm going to the *marché*."

In our village market day was only on Thursdays and was held in the town square, across from the church, a 10-minute walk from our home.

"I'll go with you."

She smiled.

I put the ukulele inside the door and closed it, took a deep satisfying breath, and smiled back.

Hand in hand, we walked up the street in the warm sunlight.

ACKNOWLEDGEMENTS

This book would not exist were it not for my wife Tiaré. She believed in it from the very beginning, when I read her the first page, and she absolutely insisted I continue writing until it was finish.

I must acknowledge my *Papa* who always encourages me in whatever endeavor I pursued, though sometimes with a quizzical look on his face; my very French *Maman*, who from an early age insisted on my having strong ties with our homeland; and my grandparents who gave me so much just by being themselves – a boy could not have had better grandparents.

There are *many* others who along the way gave significant encouragement, including Karen, Jenny and Fabrice. I thank you all.

I also have to mention Michelle, my editor and champion at 3L Publishing, who fell in love with *Feast* the first time she read it. Thanks M.

In the end, I wrote this book for that segment of society whom I hoped would read it and be moved. If you liked this book, if it touched you, well then in truth I wrote it for you.

A la vôtre,
William

ABOUT THE AUTHOR

William Widmaier has been a magazine columnist, the editor-in-chief of *The Memoirs Project*, a short story writer, and most notably a produced screenwriter.

William was born in the United States but spent many a long childhood vacation at his French grandparent's home in St. Tropez, France. Memories of these times were the foundation for the stories in *A Feast at the Beach*.